KNIGHTMARE

Hard work. No screwing around. It was how Bobby Knight went about the business of coaching his teams. The anger that fueled him—that temper that started all the way back as a kid in Orrville, Ohio—was part of his public image. Almost a trademark. Like Sinatra had a temper, so did Coach. But, in Indiana, folks always looked the other way.

Chair throws, insults, foul language, countless technical fines, fights with fans and officials—nothing mattered because he was The General, Coach, Bobby Knight—the Hoosier's Conquering Hero that delivered NCAA championships and Big Ten wins.

Until he went over the line. Until his temper finally exploded.

And his legendary reign as a college basketball supercoach ended in disgrace.

BOOK YOUR PLACE ON OUR WEBSITE AND MAKE THE READING CONNECTION!

We've created a customized website just for our very special readers, where you can get the inside scoop on everything that's going on with Zebra, Pinnacle and Kensington books.

When you come online, you'll have the exciting opportunity to:

- View covers of upcoming books
- Read sample chapters
- Learn about our future publishing schedule (listed by publication month *and author*)
- Find out when your favorite authors will be visiting a city near you
- Search for and order backlist books from our online catalog
- Check out author bios and background information
- Send e-mail to your favorite authors
- Meet the Kensington staff online
- Join us in weekly chats with authors, readers and other guests
- Get writing guidelines
- AND MUCH MORE!

Visit our website at http://www.pinnaclebooks.com

KNIGHT FALL

BOBBY KNIGHT

The Truth Behind America's
Most Controversial Coach

PHIL BERGER

PINNACLE BOOKS
KENSINGTON PUBLISHING CORP.
www.pinnaclebooks.com

PINNACLE BOOKS are published by

Kensington Publishing Corp.
850 Third Avenue
New York, NY 10022

All Kensington Titles, Imprints, and Distributed Lines are available at special quantity discounts for bulk purchases for sales promotions, premiums, fund-raising, educational, or institutional use.

Special book excerpts or customized printings can also be created to fit specific needs. For details, write or phone the office of the Kensington special sales manager: Kensington Publishing Corp., 850 Third Avenue, New York, NY 10022, attn: Special Sales Department, Phone: 1-800-221-2647

Pinnacle and the P logo Reg. U.S. Pat. & TM Off.

First Printing: September, 2000
10 9 8 7 6 5 4 3 2 1

Printed in the United States of America

For the Weekend at 8 basketball gang . . .
and our commissioner, Michael Rakosi.

Acknowledgments

My thanks to the following college sports information personnel—Todd Starowitz at Indiana, Mike Albright at Army and Steve Snapp at Ohio State—for their help in tracking Knight's past.

Andy Segman of Black Canyon Productions provided copies of pages from Knight's Orrville High School yearbooks that proved useful.

Joy Birdsong at *Sports Illustrated* allowed me access to research materials in the magazine's library for which I'm grateful.

Through the years, many publications and many fine writers have covered Bobby Knight's career. Their work gave me a through-line on the coach and mostly repudiated his assertions that journalism is work for the single-minded.

Credit to the sports staff of the *Indianapolis*

Star for being on Knight patrol full-time and ever-so-diligently.

Bruce Newman, while a student at I-U, wrote a remarkable Knight profile for the campus daily before he graduated to *Sports Illustrated.* Other Sports Illustrated writers who've covered Knight capably through the years include Pat Putnam, John Papanek, Frank Deford, Gerry Callahan and Alexander Wolff.

A nod to Mark Heisler of the Los Angeles Times for his reporting on Knight's involvement with the 1984 U.S. Olympic basketball team.

I have quoted from the book, *A Season on the Brink: A Year With Bob Knight and the Indiana Hoosiers,* which is the work of John Feinstein, a top professional.

And a special thanks to Kensington sales professional Rich Meszaros who was instrumental to the publication of this book.

Finally, thanks to those I interviewed for this book, with particular appreciation to Knight's Orrville High basketball coach, Jack Graham; his Orrville High football and baseball coach, Bill Shunkwiler and Ohio State teammate Mel Nowell.

Contents

1

Riding the Razor's Edge

It was no shock when Bobby Knight's career imploded.

For nearly three decades, as coach of Indiana University basketball, he had ruled his teams like a Parris Island drill sergeant, haranguing, cursing, prodding his players into his vision of excellence. Bobby Knight's teams worked hard, were fundamentally sound and often overachieved. They won. Year after year they won.

Friend and foe alike—and Knight had many of both—conceded he knew his business. Not only knew his business but had a passion for this boy's game that did not grow stale with age. But among both camps—his countless admirers, his legion of critics—it had been apparent for a long time that Bobby Knight was at risk.

Knight had a dark side. He could not control the fire within. He came at the world, as he came at the game of basketball, with a belly full of rage that time and again brought trouble. There was bad history with Knight—a chronology of run-ins, blow-ups, Vesuvian misbehavior. All that intensity of his had made him a ticking time bomb.

As a perpetual winner, though, he was let slide. Through the years, as he became entangled in all those "incidents," nobody at Indiana thought to reign him in. For most of his 29 years there, Knight did as Knight pleased. He was the emperor of Bloomington, reinforced in his authoritarian character by the lack of objection from on high. At Indiana University a code of silence prevailed.

Knight's most fervent supporters tended to dismiss his temper-driven misdeeds as mere lapses. They viewed Knight as a throwback—an old-fashioned disciplinarian whose tough love built character. And in an era when big-time athletic programs routinely "cheated," they could rightfully cite Knight as simon-pure. He ran a clean program. His players went to class; they graduated. They achieved success on the court and in life beyond the arena. Many of them went on to become NBA players and/or coaches on the college level and in the pro game.

There were aspects of Knight's character that even the most hard-boiled of detractors would grant were admirable. Indeed, it was that heroic potential, when set against against his bullheaded acts, that made him such an intriguing character. For within the paradox was the fuse that, once lit, could consume his career, as it had a hero of Knight's, Ohio State football coach Woody Hayes.

Knight was often compared with Hayes. Both men shared that Type A intensity about coaching; their rage often seeming disproportionate to the moment. In Hayes's case, his career had gone up in smoke when, in full view of a national TV audience, he had punched a Clemson player from the sidelines at the end of the 1978 Gator Bowl. Those who knew Knight—friends and foes alike—wondered if such a fate was in store for him. In March 1997, the *Indianapolis Star* ran a cartoon of Knight staring into a mirror and finding Hayes staring back at him.

Even close colleagues in the coaching fraternity foresaw the consequences of his wound-tight personality. As far back as 1986, Marquette coach Al McGuire had worried over his good friend Knight. In a preface to John Feinstein's *A Season on the Brink: A Year with Bob Knight and the Indiana Hoosiers,* McGuire had written these prophetic words:

Once. . . . I was at a clinic with him in
Cherry Hill, New Jersey, and I told him I
thought a day would come when he
needed to calm down at least a little, that
if he rode the razor's edge all the time the
way he did, sooner or later, he would slip
over.

Fourteen years later, it came to pass. On Sun-
day September 10, 2000, the president of Indiana
University, Dr. Myles Brand, fired the controversial coach.

The firing came 17 weeks after Brand put
Knight on notice that the coach's chronic misbehavior had to cease, or else—an ultimatum that
been prompted by a seven-week in-house investigation looking into allegations that Knight had
choked one of his players. "Zero tolerance" was
the new policy for Knight at a school that had
permitted him to run amock in previous administrations. So said Brand at a May 15th press
conference, telling media members that an apparently contrite Knight had promised to change his
ways.

But on the September day he axed Knight,
Brand would say that Knight's had been a false
promise—that from May 15th on he had shown
no readiness to change. Brand said the coach had

been "defiant and hostile" and displayed a "continued unwillingness" to work within the guidelines the university had set for him. In other words, he remained Bobby Knight—the hardcore stubborn and arrogant figure he'd always been.

The incident that would bring Knight's situation to critical mass came on September 7th on campus when a freshman student at Indiana University flippantly addressed Knight by his last name as the coach walked by. The student would claim that Knight manhandled him while giving him a lecture on civility, saying among other things, "Show me some fucking respect. I'm older than you."

Brand would say that that incident alone was not cause for firing. Rather, he said, it was part of a pattern of behavior that reflected the coach's indifference to the new rules of the game. According to Brand, during the seventeen weeks since "zero tolerance" was declared, Knight had verbally abused a high-ranking female I-U official in her office, had snubbed Alumni Club events, had uttered inflammatory comments about school officials and trustees—in short, had acted as though he was still the King Tut of coaches.

The wonder of Knight's tortured journey to

his very public, and embarrassing, dismissal was that it took so long to happen. For years—make that decades—he had been a coaching genius with a serious attitude problem. It took a televised report to trigger a chain of events that would create that seemingly inevitable headline: KNIGHT FIRED!

2

A Mad-dog Coach

It was a CNN/Sports Illustrated televised feature on Knight—a year in the making—that eventually put the coach's career in jeopardy.

CNN/SI aired its investigative segment on Knight on March 15, 2000, as the NCAA tournament was about to begin.

The profile sought to give the coach his due, a narrator saying he was "a man who has helped raise some $5 million for his university's library and [is] the object of a near fanatical devotion from his former players and from citizens throughout the state of Indiana."

A former player of Knight's, Alan Henderson—at the time a forward with the Atlanta Hawks—appeared on camera to utter a few words of praise for Knight.

But—

CNN/SI hadn't spent that year gathering hosannas for Knight. Its profile proved to be down-and-dirty, a savaging of a man it described as "intimidating . . . temperamental . . . profane . . . a coach who bullies referees, his players and the media."

An audiotape of Knight was played to offer convincing proof of the verbal abuse to which the coach subjected his troops. In the profanity-charged outburst, captured during a 1991 team practice and widely circulated on the internet, Knight was heard to say: "And then I'm leaving and you fucking guys will run until you can't eat supper. Now I am tired of this shit. I'm sick and fucking tired of an 8–10 record. I'm fucking tired of losing to Purdue. I'm not here to fuck around this week. Now you may be, but I'm not. Now I am gonna fucking guarantee you that if we don't play up there Monday night, you aren't gonna believe the next four fucking days. Now I am not here to get my ass beat on Monday. Now you better understand that right now. This is absolute fucking bullshit. Now I'll fucking run your ass right into the ground. I mean I'll fucking run you, you'll think last night was a fucking picnic. I had to sit around for a fucking year with an 8–10 record in this fucking league [The Big Ten] and I mean you will not put me in that fucking position again, or you will goddamn pay for it like you can't fucking believe."

Knight's tough talk did not constitute an idle threat. As the CNN/SI segment would allege, anger this coach and it might very well provoke him to act boorishly, brutally. Such an instance was described by former Hoosier players, Richard Mandeville and Neil Reed.

> MANDEVILLE: In our locker room there is a bathroom right attached to it and he came out, pants down around his ankles and just wiped his ass and said this is how you guys are playing.

> REED: And he just stuck his hand out with that toilet paper after he had wiped and kind of showed everyone and then walked back into the stall.

Another former Knight charge, Charlie Miller, then attempted to justify the incident, saying: "That's just his way of, I guess, you know, expressing himself. If I can't tell you, I have to show you. And what other way to show you rather than pull my pants down, wipe my ass and say you are playing like shit—that's coach Knight."

Others interviewed by CNN/SI were not inclined to let Knight off that easy. Murray Sperber, a tenured professor of English and American studies at Indiana and a long-time critic of Knight's—one of the few at the I-U campus—said, "I don't think it's acceptable for an adult. In fact, I wouldn't accept it in a child. I know that if I did it in this classroom here at Indiana, I would probably lose my tenure by the time that I got back to my office on the fourth floor. I call him the emperor of Indiana, and there is no one in this state really who will stand up to him and certainly there is no one in this university who will, and so in a sense if you are the emperor, you are allowed to do what you want. You want to wipe your ass in front of your team? Have the toilet paper, Bob."

Sperber's assertion that Knight's was a kingdom unto itself was reinforced by the claim that he had once thrown the school's president, Dr. Myles Brand, out of a practice.

REED: Coach Knight could hear him and just stopped practice and, "Goddamn, quit talking. I don't come into your office and talk while you are working. Get the hell out of here." And the president kind of looked, grabbed his stuff and walked out.

MANDEVILLE: He's kicked him out, I know that. What he said to him I'm not sure, but the president was always coming around. And he's not just kicked HIM out, he's kicked people out of practice during practice if he is pissed off or things aren't going well.

Had that been the extent of what CNN/SI uncovered, Knight probably would have been excused still again by the I-U administration and the Hoosiers' rabid followers and continued doing business as usual. Oh, his partisans might have grimaced at the foul language in his harangue of his players. Pretty hard to deny that. But as in the past, his supporters would have insisted there was a bigger picture—that like the Parris Island drill sergeant, Bobby Knight, disciplinarian, made men out of boys.

But CNN/SI had one other instance of Knight's misbehavior that would trump the other allegations—Neil Reed's claim that Knight had choked him during a practice.

Reed, a schoolboy All America guard from East Jefferson High in Metairie, Louisiana, had started 72 games for Indiana, averaging just under 10 points a game. The son of a coach, he was a scrappy, intelligent player. But in 1997, as a junior, he had run afoul of Knight.

As a season would progress, Knight, who vented his anger at all his players, might choose one or two of them to hammer without letup—scapegoat the poor bastards beyond apparent reason. Sometimes it might be a star, like Steve Alford, whom he deepdown admired and felt could "take" his baiting. But there were other times when Knight's rancor would turn corrosive—would cease being a psychological ploy and get downright personal. It was what Reed claimed happened between Knight and him.

Reed said the turning point came during a practice when Knight got on him for not alerting a teammate that a pass was coming to him. When Reed insisted he had shouted a heads-up, Knight asked the teammate in question, Larry Richardson. According to the CNN/SI report, Richardson said Reed had shouted to him.

> REED: At that point, coach thrust right at me, just came right at me, wasn't far away enough to where I couldn't see it coming, was close enough to come at me and reach and put his hand around my throat. He came at me with two hands but grabbed me with one hand.

Reed said that Knight had choked him for about five seconds and that assistant coaches Dan

Dakich and Ron Felling had to pull Knight off him. CNN reported that it had corroborated the incident with three other sources who declined to have their names used or to be on camera. Whatever. From that moment, Reed said, he fell into disfavor with Knight and became the coach's "whipping boy."

At the end of his junior year, Reed said that Knight told him he would not get to play as a senior, a threat that prompted the player to transfer to Southern Mississippi. He finished his varsity career there and then played professionally in the Netherlands for a season before, as CNN/SI put it, "deciding his heart was no longer in basketball."

On March 14, 2000, a day before the Knight segment was to be aired, CNN/SI had issued a press release promoting it.

Later that day, Indiana University convened a press conference in response. Todd Starowitz, the acting men's basketball media relations director, told newsmen that he believed the timing of the report—on the eve of the NCAA tournament (Indiana was to play Pepperdine)—was "calculated," and not, as Steve Robinson, managing editor of CNN/SI, had asserted in that day's edition of *USA Today*, simply because the reporting was concluded.

"To give you some of the background on the story itself," Starowitz said, "I was contacted by a few different players who had played here previously, who said that CNN/SI had been contacting them for upwards of a year. They said that several of them had spoken to a producer at CNN who had gone down the road of a lot of negative questions, and that they thought they were fishing for some different things. They called and just didn't feel comfortable with it, and just wanted to make us aware of the tone of some of the questions. At that point, I called, probably about two months ago, just to inquire about the story, and they were very defensive and said, 'Well, this is CNN. We'll certainly do a balanced story. We will ask for a response from Indiana.'

"At that time they sent over a fax requesting Coach Knight's rebuttal and response, and also mentioned the players that they had spoken to previously, who were Neil Reed and other players who had left under terms not necessarily on their own, guys that had transferred and things of that nature. Certainly at that point we felt like that they were certainly going to be an attacking story and Coach declined to comment to them. Which led to them saying, essentially, that Coach

Knight's denial to speak to CNN is an admission of guilt, which is totally false."

Starowitz then read statements from university president Brand, from Dakich (now head basketball coach at Bowling Green State University), from team trainer Tim Garl and from former player Robbie Eggers (1995–98) in which all the incidents described in the CNNSI report were denied.

Then two players on Knight's NCAA-bound squad, All-American A. J. Guyton and Mike Lewis, appeared before newsmen to add their denials while maligning Mandeville and especially Reed.

Guyton characterized Reed as a selfish player and added: "Guys that have transferred from here and had reasons for transferring from here—such as Coach verbally and physically abusing you— show that you haven't developed into a man. I think that's the main reason why Neil Reed is coming out with these statements at the wrong time."

Lewis depicted Reed as a whiner who never accepted blame, and insisted that Reed had not left I-U on his own accord but had been voted off the team by the rest of the squad.

"I never saw Coach grab Neil around the neck or choke him in any way," said Lewis. "He'll move players into position. He's grabbed me by the waist and put me in a position or put me in a stance. But I've never seen Coach touch anybody or grab anybody in any way trying to physically harm them."

Deny, deny, deny. That would be the approach that Knight and the I-U administration would take in the days and weeks that followed CNN/SI's report. It was a tried-and-tested approach, one that had made other Knight-provoked "situations" go away. But damage control was not limited to simple denial. The Knight defense sought to scuff up the opposition.

Questioning the journalistic integrity of CNNSI, Starowitz said, "We had heard from other people besides our players, other people who had actually worked at CNNSI that CNNSportsIllustrated had said that the producer and other people involved in the piece had had it out for Coach Knight for upwards of 15 years, back actually to when Indiana played North Carolina in the NCAA tournament in 1984."

But more than CNN/SI, Neil Reed remained the target of choice for the coach's apologists. Reed, who as a freshman at I-U had played most of the season with a separated shoulder, now suddenly was depicted as a wuss, a crybaby, an outcast. He hadn't the right stuff, couldn't take the discipline that Knight used to build his players. He wasn't a man.

Yet back when Reed had been a starter with the Hoosiers, Knight had praised him for his grittiness, saying: "We're not tough at any position on our team with the exception of Neil Reed. He's a tough kid, but with everyone else there's a toughness that's lacking."

But now a revisionist view of Reed was propounded. Players like Guyton, Lewis, Robbie Eggers, even trainer Tim Garl, insisted the choking incident never happened. The Hoosiers' athletic department made public a letter in which Reed was accused of using foul language at Knight's summer camp by the mother of a camper. And I-U defenders of Knight reiterated that Reed hadn't left Bloomington on his own accord—he had been banished, voted off the team by teammates who saw him for what he was.

Well, *Sports Illustrated*'s basketball-savvy Alexander Wolff would insist that that scenario was sheer propaganda. In a column written for CNN/SI.com he reported that the so-called vote occurred after Knight had told Reed—a junior at the time—that he would not play his senior year and Reed then quit the team. "Knight asked the remaining players to vote on (crucial distinction here) whether they'd take Reed back if he changed his mind. According to several sources, the first ballot was yea, though not unanimous. Only after Knight resubmitted the proposal—having made clear the outcome he wanted to see—did the vote swing to 8–0 against Reed."

Wolff would view the character assassination of Reed as the work of Knight's "yes men" and depict the coach as a kind of puppetmaster pulling their strings. Wolf called him an autocrat. Others in the press had worse to say about Knight in the aftermath of the CNN/SI report.

The bad press was no surprise. Knight had antagonized the fourth estate from early in his tenure at Indiana, treating it with an air of disdain—and ridiculing reporters as mental midgets.

"As a kid," he once said, "I wanted to be a political cartoonist because you only need one idea a day. But then I decided to be a sportswriter because you don't need any ideas."

On another occasion, he noted, "Most of us learn to write in the second or third grade and then go on to other things."

A *New York Times* columnist would report Knight at a press conference saying, "I'll answer all your questions except for those from that hunchback from Louisville"—a reference to a reporter who had written critically of him and who in fact did have a slight physical deformity.

And then there was the time when, addressing a luncheon in Dayton, Ohio, Knight said, "Let's have ten seconds of silence to give the sportswriters in attendance something they can quote accurately."

As columnist Rick Reilly later observed: "Knight being civil to a sportswriter is like a Doberman being civil to a pork chop."

But it wasn't simply payback that provoked the hard line many in the press took. Knight offended their sense of decency. To more than a few of them, he seemed like nothing more than a classic bully, a nasty son of a bitch—and arrogant to boot. The quintessential Knight, they would tell you, was exposed on a seniors' night in 1994 when, in pre-game praise of his graduating players, Coach stood at the microphone and detoured with these words aimed at his detractors: "When my time on earth is done, and my activities here are past, I want them to bury me upside down and my critics can kiss my ass."

That was Knight, taking what should have been a sentimental tribute to players who had withstood four years of his unrelenting harangues and turning it into a referendum about his long-simmering discontent with the media. "I didn't think [the poem] was particularly necessary," he conceded later. "It just struck me as something that would entertain me a little bit."

Instead it appalled his critics, and even some friends. But with Bobby Knight, that was how it went. In the end, it was always about Bobby Knight.

Even in Indiana, where Knight was revered by the public, the party line was breached by the press. Bill Benner, a columnist with the *Indianapolis Star,* was often critical of the coach, a perspective that incited many of his readers—the hard-core defenders of the faith.

Wrote Benner after the CNN/SI segment had been aired: "I've been threatened, and I understand other threats have been posted [on the internet]. Given the world as it is now, I do not take these threats lightly."

A sampling from those irate readers:

—"I hope you rot in hell you bastard and if I see you crossing the street, I won't hit the brakes."

—"Your column is first-class shit."

—"Bob Knight comes from the old school and he kicks butt and takes names and there's a lot of people out there like that, including me. There's a lot of us who come up years ago and if you had a kid, you jerked him in line and got his attention. You obviously should have had your ass kicked a few times."

—"Bob Knight lives and he rules. Fuck you."

It wasn't just Knight, though, that the media went after. The school itself became a target, accused of being Knight's enabler through the 29 years he had been coach. As the furor kicked up by CNN/SI begat a hailstorm of negative commentary from newspapers, magazines and internet sites across the country, the I-U administration began to feel the heat.

The school was uneasy with the assault on its standards, the suggestion that it no longer lived up to its motto—"Lux et veritas" (light and truth) —but instead rolled over for the big bucks and the high profile that Knight-coached teams— three of them NCAA champions—had generated.

On March 23, 2000, I-U president Brand announced that the school would conduct an investigation of Knight, and named two members of the board of trustees, John Walda and Frederick Eichhorn, Jr., both attorneys, to head the probe. At this point, the major issue was whether the coach had choked Neil Reed.

"Any time a student athlete raises questions of physical abuse by a coach, it is a serious matter," said Brand in a statement. "Once charges of this nature have been raised, we are obligated to review the matter."

But how authentic an investigation would this be? Brand's decision to use trustees instead of outside investigators was viewed skeptically by some newsmen, who wondered aloud about his appointment of Walda, for earlier Walda had gone on record as saying that he "would put no stock" in Reed's claim that Coach had choked him. The same skeptics pointed to an article for the op-ed page of the *Indianapolis Star* that Brand and Walda had co-authored in February 1998, in response to criticism of Knight. The article appeared after a game in which Knight had raged at a referee, been assessed three technical fouls and been subsequently fined $10,000 by the Big Ten Conference for unsportsmanlike conduct. Walda and Brand wrote:

> Strong emotion in athletics, both among players and coaches, is understandable and even productive, provided it does not cross the line of reasonable behavior. Some coaches have crossed that line. One example is Woody Hayes. . . . But Ohio State acted correctly in dismissing Hayes when he crossed the line by striking a player.
>
> Knight demands much of his players and himself; and when there are avoidable mistakes, he lets his feelings be known—sometimes in a way that comes across as

excessive. But he knows the limits of reasonable action.

If Brand's intention was to whitewash Knight, as administrations preceding his had whenever the coach got in a jam, events would conspire to force the Indiana University trustees to conduct a more than cursory investigation. The CNN/SI report would turn out to be a mere starting point. Soon after Brand announced the school's plans to investigate the Reed accusation, other revelations of unsavory behavior by Knight would surface, leaving the trustees no choice but to widen the scope of their investigation.

On Thursday March 29, the *Indianapolis Star* broke a story, headlined "KNIGHT HAD ALTERCATION WITH BOSS," in which it reported that Knight had gone ballistic on Indiana's athletic director, Clarence Doninger, after a February 19 loss to Ohio State. Doninger, a member of the 1957 I-U Big Ten champion basketball team and part of the winning squad in the Little 500—the bicycle race featured in the film *Breaking Away*—had told Knight "tough loss," intending the words to console the coach. But in the hallways outside the I-U dressing room, the temperamental Knight reacted as if the sentiment expressed was a provocation. He berated Doninger, who later said he felt physically threatened. The *Star* reported that team doctor Brad Bomba had to step in to break up the altercation and that Knight's son, Pat, an assistant coach at the time, also had to be restrained. Doninger was so shaken by the encounter that he reported it to a university vice-president.

On the surface, the outburst by Knight seemed totally irrational. But by Knight's way of seeing things, it wasn't. Doninger, who had represented Knight in his mid-1980s divorce from his first wife, Nancy Lou, had long been regarded as an ally of the coach. But reportedly Knight became disenchanted with Doninger when the athletic director failed to support him after a public altercation with a stranger outside a restaurant the previous June. It was not the first time—nor would it be the last—when Knight had disenfranchised a friend for failing to walk lock-step with him on every issue of importance to him. There were no shades of gray with "The General," as the coach was known.

As the Doninger brouhaha faded, more dark revelations about Knight would surface. For three seasons in the eighties, Ricky Calloway, a six-foot-six forward, had averaged double figures for Knight and had been a key player on Indiana's NCAA-champion team in 1986–87. But after his junior year, 1987–88, Calloway, apparently weary of Knight's methods, had transferred to Kansas. Now, as he watched from afar the organized smear campaign against Neil Reed, he decided to speak up.

Calloway told the *Houston Chronicle* that Knight had been physical with other players—punching guard Steve Alford during a practice and slapping forward Daryl Thomas.

In the *Chronicle* story, Calloway said, "We were all standing in a circle one day, and he [Knight] just turned around and punched Steve right in the stomach, and for a minute and a half Steve couldn't breathe.

"I was shocked. I wasn't really surprised he hit someone, but I never expected him to hit Steve, his golden child. But Steve put up with a lot."

Alford, the University of Iowa coach whose once-close relationship with Knight had grown shaky, denied the incident had happened, as Calloway predicted he would. So did Thomas. Deny, deny, deny. In spite of all the dirt being dug up, Knight appeared still to be a protected figure. Knight loyalists denied and denigrated. The university investigation was headed by a man partial to the coach's cause. A rally by Indiana University fans in support of Knight was convened. A betting man would have said Bobby Knight was home free.

But then—a startling twist in the Knight saga. It turned out that there was a tape of the very practice in which Knight was said to have choked Neil Reed.

3

The Reed Tape

On April 11th, 2000, CNN/SI aired the tape.

As an *Indianapolis Star* editorial noted: "The videotape is clear. Indiana University basketball coach Bob Knight clutched Neil Reed's throat with enough force that the player's head snapped back."

The tape did not conform to every detail of Reed's account. Knight's throat grab had lasted two to three seconds, not the five seconds of Reed's version. No assistant coaches had intervened, as Reed had remembered it. But—the video was clear. Knight had lied, and so had those players who had supported his story. Bobby Knight had grabbed Reed by the throat and walked him backward a couple of steps before taking away his hand. There was no sound on the tape, but Knight appeared to be shouting at Reed.

The *Bloomington Herald-Times,* which tended to take Knight's side in his endless controversies, would use mitigating language in describing what the tape showed. Its news account had Knight "placing his right hand in the vicinity of Reed's neck."

But the time for euphemisms had passed. The trustees looking into Knight's case had flown to Atlanta to view the tape. Their preview of it altered the tone—and scope—of their investigation. From this point on, the probe would widen. Knight's pattern of repeated misbehavior would now be explored.

In the aftermath of the tape's airing, the question was raised of how CNN/SI had come into possession of it. The story that emerged would reinforce the image of a Bobby Knight gone amock. For the man who reportedly gave the tape to CNN/SI was Ron Felling, an athletic department administrative assistant who had been an assistant coach to Knight's for 12 years. Felling's I-U career had abruptly ended earlier that season when, on December 4, 1999, it was announced that he had retired.

But as Felling would later advise the trustees, he had not retired—he had been fired by Knight.

What prompted the disruption of their long-time association? Well, the story went that following a November 30th Indiana victory over Notre Dame, Knight had ripped into his squad in his postgame remarks. The following day, when former Hoosier player and assistant coach Dan Dakich phoned Felling and asked about the game, Felling characterized Knight's verbal assault on the team as taking the fun out of the game.

What neither Felling nor Dakich knew was that Knight was listening in on the conversation from an extension. Knight cut in and told Felling he was disloyal, and for that he was fired. When Felling came by Knight's office moments later to discuss their difference, Knight leaped from his seat and punched Felling, driving him back into a bookshelf of videos.

Felling, 60, would later sue Knight and the school for $1 million for negligence, negligent supervision and age discrimination. At the time his suit became public, his role as the source of the tape would be confirmed by a former Knight player, Steve Downing, who was now an associate athletic director at I-U. Downing said that Felling had told him he had kept the tape since 1997 for possible use as his "trump card."

Whatever.

Knight, it was now clear, was the object of

keen scrutiny. No whitewash this time. Indiana University was on the spot. As an editorial in the *Star* had observed, "the reputation of the university as a whole" was at stake.

What's more, the CNN/SI report in March had inspired other victims of Knight's excesses to speak out and had encouraged investigative journalism. The floodgates had opened. As April turned to May, more reports of Knight's misbehavior surfaced.

On May 11, 2000, the facts behind the Felling firing were revealed by television station WTHR in Indianapolis.

On the same day, the *Indianapolis Star* reported that in the 1970s Knight had choked and punched Indiana's longtime sports information director, Kit Klingelhofer, over a news release that upset the coach.

A day later, the *Star* had an even more disturbing revelation. Athletic director Doninger's secretary, Jeanette Hartgraves, now 66, said that in February 1998, a secretary of Knight's had called, requesting Knight be put through to an individual who at that moment was conferring with Doninger. When Hartgraves asked if she could pass word on what Knight wanted, the coach had gotten on the phone and told her it was "none of your fucking business" before slamming down the phone.

Moments later, Hartgraves said, Knight appeared in the waiting area of Doninger's office, called her "a fucking bitch" and was moving toward her in anger when Doninger stepped out of his office and intervened.

It was not Hartgraves's only unpleasant encounter with the coach. In the late 1980s, as secretary to an earlier I-U athletic director, Ralph Floyd, Hartgraves said that an angry Knight had thrown a potted plant against the wall, shattering the ceramic pot and a glass picture frame, pieces of which hit her, though they did not cause injury.

The trustees also learned about an altercation Knight had had with his son Tim, 35, a 1986 graduate of Stanford University. Tim Knight had suffered a dislocated shoulder and a broken nose in a May 1994 scuffle with his father. The incident had occurred during a hunting trip north of Buenos Aires, Argentina, when an argument between father and sons (Patrick and Tim) turned physical.

Tim would insist that the incident was an aberration—that he and Coach got along just fine. In fact, Tim, the older of the two Knight boys, handled some of his father's business affairs, booking his dad for speeches, clinics, promotional appearances—a rich source of the coach's handsome earnings.

And then there had been an allegation in a book written by a former I-U player, Toronto Raptor coach Buch Carter, that during a practice Knight had directed a racial slur at his teammate Isiah Thomas. Thomas would deny the charge, but the cumulation of the revelations no longer could be ignored.

Like the Watergate break-in, which Republicans initially had labeled a penny-ante burglary but which had gathered a momentum that in time would sully the reputation of Richard Nixon and chase him from office, so now did the CNN/SI report appear to be working up similar momentum to dislodge the coach.

Bobby Knight, for nearly three decades the high priest of "Hoosier Hysteria," as the phenomenon of basketball was referred to in Indiana, once had been so widely admired in the state that his behavioral excesses were routinely condoned by a public and an I-U administration that doted on his success. As the new millennium unfolded, Knight had won three NCAA titles and 11 Big Ten championships, and had a lifetime total of 763 victories. Given license to continue at Indiana, he figured to become the winningest Division I coach ever, overtaking North Carolina's Dean Smith, who had retired with a career record total of 879 victories.

The thought of the often-abrasive Knight surpassing the widely-admired, gentlemanly Smith roused *Sports Illustrated* columnist Rick Reilly to write that it "would be akin to Jerry Springer's winning a Pulitzer. Knight ahead of Dean Smith? As a man, Knight can't carry Smith's whistle."

No matter. Only a month before, in mid-April, as supporters of Knight rallied out front of Assembly Hall, the home court of the Hoosiers, to praise him publicly, he still appeared to be Teflon Bob—a coach to whom nothing nasty stuck. On that day the Knight faithful wore signs that said "The Lord is my Shepherd, and Knight is my coach," and "We're Knight going to take it anymore." Players of his from past and present teams praised the coach, and statements in support of Knight from coaching friends like Tony LaRussa and Bill Parcells were read to the partisan crowd.

In Philadelphia, Temple's coach, John Chaney, told newsmen that Knight was being victimized by media that tended to offer only the sensationalized "snapshots," not the bigger picture.

"If people took snapshots of my program, it might look even worse," he said. "We set up all types of situations in a gym that fans wouldn't accept. People can argue about our methods, but we are measured by our deeds to the majority of youngsters we deal with.

"Great programs take a bigger hit when someone peeks in the keyhole and walks away with a snapshot. The outsiders should just deal with the product and not at how we arrive at it, how we develop young men. It would be like me telling you how to raise your kids in your house. These hate-mongers see that one little opening to put a foot on some one's head. It's not what have you done in the past. It's what have you done for me lately."

Indeed, there had been a slight erosion of support for Knight in his own backyard—the predictable result of a decline in I-U's success, most notably during the NCAA tournament. In March, Pepperdine had demolished Indiana 77–57, continuing a trend of Hoosier teams failing in the early rounds of the postseason tournament—two wins in the past six seasons. It had been 13 years since Indiana's last NCAA championship team, in 1987.

Knight's detractors put the team's NCAA-tournament failures to the toll the coach's non-stop pressure took on players. Knight wore the boys out emotionally—and more: He made them so fraught with fear-of-Coach that they froze in the big games. Rather than rely on instinct, the players worried about making mistakes that would incur the coach's wrath. So the thinking of these fans went.

Increasingly grass-roots critics had begun to surface, wondering aloud whether the game had passed Knight by—was he out of touch with the sort of player that now was coming up, and around which basketball programs were built. In an era of intense recruiting, where blue-chip players were identified earlier and had their egos massaged liberally, the graduating high school athlete who emerged tended to be a self-absorbed sort—shoot first and then ask questions. This was precisely the opposite of the team-oriented player with the wide-screen view of the game that Knight had recruited.

In 1997, former Hoosier player Pat Graham summed it up this way: "He still wants the kid he got in the '70s, the hard-nosed gritty player. The problem is there are far fewer of those kids today than there used to be."

Added another I-U player from the '90s, Todd Lindeman: "Coach Knight hasn't changed; I just don't think kids want to go through the demands of his program any more. They're all thinking they're going to play in the NBA. They've got other options, and they're just not ready for his strict procedures."

Yet even if the typical elite player was now anathema to Coach Bob, and even if a small percentage of I-U faithful questioned his ability,

Knight still reigned supreme at I-U. At least until April 11, the night CNN/SI showed that tape of Knight clutching Reed by the throat. From that moment on, like Nixon before him, the coach would be under siege, the shift in momentum obvious, even to him.

On April 13, just days after the "choking" tape was exposed, the *Indiana Daily Student*, a campus newspaper, had called for Knight's ouster in an editorial:

> Championship glory has never excused national embarrassment and player abuse. It is about time university officials realized that. . . . No matter how many titles Knight has won, no matter how much money he brings into the university, and no matter how many players he graduates—the end has never justified the means.

That was just the beginning of the onslaught. Knight needed no crystal ball, no tea leaves to fathom his situation. For the first time in nearly three decades as coach of Indiana University, he had lost his leverage. His job was in jeopardy. And so, on May 13, 2000, two days before President Brand's announcement of what he and the trustees had decided to do about their controversial coach, with his second wife, Karen, accompanying him, Bobby Knight made his way to Bryan House, Brand's campus residence. He was about to do what only months before would have seemed unthinkable: Robert Montgomery Knight was going to beg for his job.

For the coach, this would mark a radical detour on the long road he had traveled, all the way from small-town obscurity in Ohio.

4

Big Boy of the Red Riders

The town of Orrville, located in northeastern Ohio, was an unassuming little place, a railway crossroads hunkered down between New York and Chicago. In post-World War I America, Orrville served as a stopping point for America's bustling rail traffic as it flowed east and west. Folks from Cleveland or Akron were obliged to catch a spur line to Orrville in order to hook up with the Broadway Limited.

Carroll Knight—known as Pat to his friends—had come to Orrville from Oklahoma and gone to work for the Nickel Plate Railroad as a freight agent, his job to make sure that the flatcars that rumbled into Orrville empty left fully loaded and on time. He would work there until he suffered a heart attack in 1962.

In 1934, when Pat Knight was 37, he married Hazel Henthorne, 31, a grade-school teacher who lived in Akron but taught in Orrville. Their only child, Robert Montgomery Knight, was born October 25, 1940, a couple of weeks before Franklin Delano Roosevelt won his third term over Wendell Willkie and over the objections of the conservative Orrville electorate.

Orrville, population 5,000, was Norman Rockwell America—a small town with a water tower and playgrounds and the sweet scent of apple butter wafting through its streets from the Smucker's Jam factory.

The locals were church-goers—five churches clustered in the heart of the town: Methodist, Presbyterian, Evangelical and Reformed, Lutheran and Mennonite—and they were family-oriented. The citizens of Orrville worked hard, saved their money and said their prayers at night.

Pat Knight had a severe hearing problem, and it limited the communication between father and son. At night, when he returned home from work, he would turn off his hearing aid and read the evening paper from cover to cover. He was not a loquacious, or outgoing individual. Yet while Bobby's contact with his father was not storybook warm, he admired the old man for his straightforward manner.

His father was principled, to a degree that made an impression on his son. Never one to buy on time, Pat Knight made an exception for the Knights' one-story house at 714 North Vine Street—a 20-year mortgage that he then paid off in four and half years by denying himself golf and other pleasures.

"My father," said Bobby Knight, "was the most disciplined man I ever saw. Most people, they hear the word discipline, and right away they think about a whip and a chair. I've worked up my own definition. And this took a long time. Discipline: doing what you have to do, and doing it as well as you possibly can, and doing it that way all the time."

Pat Knight was tough, stubborn and direct. "Brutally tough," recalled Bobby. "One time in winter, leaving for work, he slipped on the ice, and he threw his right hand up behind his head so he didn't crack his head on the steps, then picked himself up and went to work. And when he came home from work, his arm was in a cast because he'd broken both bones in his wrist. And he'd spent all day working, writing left-handed, then went to see the doctor after work."

By all accounts, Knight drew emotional succor from his maternal grandmother, Sarah Henthorne, who lived with the family at their North

Vine Street home and doted on the boy. "Henthorne"—all her friends called her by her last
name—supported the boy in all his pursuits and
gave him time and unconditional love.

"I think he was closer to her than he ever was
to me or his father," Hazel Henthorne would say.
"There wasn't a night that he didn't go into her
room when he got home and kiss her good
night."

Bobby Knight was a bright youngster, earning
A's in his schoolwork, even the second-grade
curriculum taught by his mother. From early on,
he was a boy who liked reading. He pored over
biographies and books on history and developed
a love for a series of 23 inspirational sports novels revolving around a high school boy named
Chip Hilton. The series, which was written by a
college basketball coach named Clair Bee of
Long Island University—who was later to become one of Knight's coaching mentors, usually
raised moral issues that the wholesome Chip—
sometimes with the help of his widowed mom
and/or the straightshooting Coach Rockwell—
would overcome.

"My parents," recalled Knight, "used to
make one trip a week to Akron, the closest big
town, about 20 miles from Orrville. When I got
to be 15, I balked at making that long trip. But

they got me to go by saying I could buy a Chip Hilton book. I'd go to O'Neill's department store and there'd be stacks of Nancy Drew and the Hardy Boys and Chip Hilton. I'd stand there half a day picking out the Chip Hilton I wanted. I still have all those books."

Knight was tall for his age, and athletic. He experienced early success as a baseball player. A natural at the game, he spent long hours on the sandlots of Orrville, marathon contests that he never tired of. "I remember batting in the bottom of the 45th inning with the score 129–123 and we just kept playing hard every inning."

By the fifth grade, he was persuaded to try basketball. Although he would continue to play other sports, basketball soon became his passion. Years later, he would write about the game's hold on him, saying, "Basketball is the All American and the All-Pro: it's a ragtag kid shooting a worn-out ball through a broken rim; it's the guy who plays 40 minutes and the guy who just hopes to get in the game. Basketball . . . is long hours of practice before empty stands. It's adulation and recognition; it's a coach hollering after every mistake. It's joy, ecstasy and triumph, but it can also be sadness, sorrow and dejection.

"Basketball is America. It's national championships and three-on-three in the schoolyards.

It's rich people and poor people; it's black people and white people; it's big people and little people."

Because he was big for his age, as a sixth grader he was invited to play with the older boys. By the eighth grade, he had grown to six foot two inches and was averaging 29 points per game in junior high games that lasted only 24 minutes.

He was dedicated to basketball, practicing late into the night at Orr Park, a lighted outdoor facility, or in the high school gym whose windows he would unlatch so that he could sneak in there on weekends to work on his jumper—an unorthodox low-trajectory shot. Wherever he went, winter or summer, he had his basketball with him. He even carried his ball with him on dates, on the chance that a game might materialize.

The dedication, and his hard work, paid off. By the ninth grade, Knight was a member of coach Jack Graham's varsity basketball squad at Orrville High School. "I was afraid," he said, "the older players would resent my being on the team, but they didn't seem to mind."

A year later, as a sophomore on a team of upperclassmen, Knight was Orrville's best player. He would lead the 8–11 Red Riders in scoring with a 19.4 points per game average and in rebounds with 15 per game.

Orrville was a small school, with a limited pool of athletic talent—some 200 boys. Knight had the size and physical skills that made Orrville High football coach, Bill Shunkwiler, believe that Bobby could be an asset for Red Rider varsity football. Shunkwiler, who coached varsity baseball too, had watched Knight as a ninth grader excel as his team's first baseman.

"He had all kinds of potential in baseball," said Shunkwiler. "He had great eye-hand coordination. He could run well, and could always hit. He had a quick bat. He was one of the few boys who could hit [future major leaguer] Dean Chance, who played for Northwestern High. Had he wanted to, Bobby could have played baseball in college, he was that good."

But when Shunkwhiler tried to recruit Knight for football, he encountered resistance. Knight knew Shunkwiler had a policy of not allowing his players to entertain other sports during the football season, which meant that Bobby would not be able to work on his basketball game.

"In those days, my policy was one sport at a time," said Shunkwiler. "But I made a deal with Bobby—I told him he could shoot on his own any time he wanted to—we just wouldn't mention it to anybody. So Bobby came out for football, and played offensive and defensive end. After football practice, he'd go home and eat, then show up at Orr Park and shoot under the lights."

In his junior year, Knight—now grown to six-feet-four, the biggest man on the team—once again dominated Red Rider basketball. Typical was his performance against Rittman High, in the team's seventh game of the season. In a 59–57 double overtime victory, Knight would score 33 points, including the game-winning 20-foot jumper five seconds into the sudden-death second overtime period.

From the news account of the game:

Knight displayed remarkable coolness under pressure, coming through with all 10 Red Rider overtime markers. In addition, the tall junior . . . had a hot night [and] scored more points than the rest of the team combined.

Through 10 games, Knight was averaging 25.5 points per game when it was discovered that he had suffered a hairline fracture of the metatarsus of his left foot. A photo of Knight in a local paper shows him sitting with a rueful expression on a home sofa. The caption beneath the photo reads: "BOBBY KNIGHT, O.H.S. Cage Star/ . . . time, not desire mends broken bones."

The story accompanying the photo would note that Knight was thinking of having an aluminum support fashioned that would permit him to continue playing.

> Bobby, who lives for basketball and would rather play than eat, is at this point quite depressed and very unhappy as he faces one of the tests of maturity.
>
> Emerging from this episode he may be a potentially greater athlete or a crushed and disappointed high school boy.
>
> It will be up to the big boy with the cast on his foot.

The big boy would make it back to the lineup late in the season and, though he played in only 12 of Orrville's 19 games, would be voted the team's Most Valuable Player. Averaging 24.3 points per game for the 5–13 Red Riders, he would look forward to his final basketball season at Orrville.

But Knight's senior year would be marked by controversy. In his three varsity basketball seasons, Knight had developed a close relationship with coach Jack Graham. When Graham went out of town to scout opposition teams, Knight—a student of the game—would volunteer to go with him.

"This started when he was a ninth grader," said Graham. "I'd keep charts, and he'd help. We'd talk about the other team's strong points and weak points. He just loved the game."

The coach and his star player also went fishing together.

"We'd go to a place outside of Bloomington," said Graham, "and fish for bass."

At the end of Knight's junior year, Graham left Orrville High to become principal of the Walnut Street Elementary School, where Hazel Knight taught second grade. Bobby would miss Graham. The new coach at Orrville was Bob Gobin, a man with whom Knight would clash almost immediately.

Gobin, whose background was in recreation, hadn't the hard-core attitude toward winning that most coaches did. He saw high school sports as an activity to involve all those who wanted to participate—no more, no less. That deemphasis struck at the heart of Knight's intense feeling for the game. What's more, it diminished his role, and his impact, as the Red Riders' star and captain. Rather than let Knight dominate, as he was capable of, Gobin would keep him in check, replacing him in the middle of a scoring tear so that another player could have a chance.

Knight had a healthy ego, as most star players

do, and already had shown flashes of a temper that would grow more volatile later on. While he was close with Shunkwiler and Graham, both coaches had had to discipline him in the years before Gobin showed up. Graham recalled an earlier run-in at a practice where he'd sent an impudent Knight to the showers. A contrite Knight caught up with him afterward.

"I told him," said Graham, " 'There's only one guy who's boss and that's me. If you understand that, we won't have any problems.' He said he understood."

As for Shunkwiler, on a bus trip to a preseason football training camp up near Lake Erie, a Trojan rubber had floated downwind, into the coach's lap. Shunkwiler decided the prank was the work of the team's leading wise guy, Bobby Knight, and he made Knight scrimmage 92 straight plays in the intense summer heat.

There was more. As a sophomore Knight had accumulated a grade-point average entitling him to be chosen for the National Honor Society. But that temper of his dissuaded his teachers from nominating him.

It wasn't just his teachers and coaches who saw evidence of an attitude. Ray Gerhart, a three-sport athlete at Orrville, remembered that if a fielder didn't make his throw perfect to first-baseman Knight, an annoyed Bobby would let the rightfielder shag after it.

By Gerhart's view, Knight was strictly-for-Bobby.

As his senior season at Orrville wound down, Knight became increasingly agitated by Bob Gobin's casual approach. Knight let Gobin know how he felt. The confrontations led, eventually, to Gobin's tossing his star off the team. Fearing that the enmity between player and coach could damage Knight's chances of landing an athletic scholarship, Bobby, his father Pat and a close friend and next-door neighbor, a dentist named Donald Boop, huddled with Gobin at his home to see if they could right the situation. The upshot was that Knight was suspended for a game and that Gobin said he would make victory more of a priority. Knight ended up averaging 24 points per game as the Red Riders made the state playoffs for the first time in years.

"To this day," said Boop, "I think it was a case of Bobby knowing more about basketball than the coach did. When it came time to vote for the team's most valuable player in his senior year, Gobin wouldn't let the team vote for Bobby because he had won the year before—even though he led the team in almost every statistical category."

The season proved to be so unsatisfying to Knight that rather than re-up with the Red Rider baseball team, he barnstormed with an all-star basketball team that spring.

Knight would graduate from Orrville, class of '58, having won ten varsity letters—4 in basketball and 3 each in baseball and football. He ranked eighth academically in a class of 80.

While at Orrville, he was recruited by several small Ohio colleges. At these schools, Knight—with his deadly shot and court awareness—would have been assured of liberal playing time. But Knight believed he had the right stuff to prosper at a Division I powerhouse. So as his father sent him on into the world with this advice, "Never gamble and don't hang out with queers," Knight accepted a basketball scholarship to Ohio State, 100 miles down the road in Columbus.

Anticipating continuing glory, he would encounter wholesale disappointment.

5

The Brat from Orrville

By 1959–60 NCAA rules, freshmen were not eligible to play varsity sports.

So Bobby Knight settled in with the Buckeye freshman team, an aggregate that was so potent, so dominant, that it captured the imagination of fans and press alike. As the frosh steamrollered opposition, it was nicknamed "The Fabulous Five."

Of course, in those days, the Buckeye freshmen did not play against freshmen teams from other schools. When the varsity would play, The Fabulous Five would go up against the Ohio State reserves—in effect, the jayvees—in the preliminary game.

Besides Knight, the freshman starters were

Gary Gearhart, Mel Nowell, Jerry Lucas and John Havlicek.

Three of those baby Buckeyes would go on to play in the pros.

Nowell, a six-foot-two guard, would see limited NBA action with the 1962–63 Chicago Bulls—39 games, a 5.9 points per game average—and then play a season in the ABA with New Jersey—76 games, a 9.5 points per game average.

The six-foot-eight Lucas would fare far better. He would play 11 NBA seasons with Cincinnati, San Francisco and New York, averaging 17 points per game while doing yeoman work as a rebounder. Seven times he would be named to the All-Star game.

Havlicek—a six-foot-five perpetual-motion aggressor known as "Hondo"—would become one of the game's all-time greats in 16 seasons as a Boston Celtic, averaging 20.8 points per game and acquiring a reputation for making the clutch play. Thirteen times he would be named to the All-Star game.

As the frosh routinely pounded the jayvees and defeated the varsity in a game, it was widely thought that the Fabulous Five would step up to varsity play intact—that the entire quintet would comprise coach Fred Taylor's starting lineup over their final three years. The frosh were that good.

But Taylor would not go that route. For the 1959–60 season, he would mix and match his best freshman—Havlicek, Lucas and Nowell—with holdovers Larry Siegfried and Joe Roberts, both of whom would also have pro careers.

The six-foot-six Roberts would play three seasons with the Syracuse Nationals in the NBA, averaging 6.2 points per game, before a final year with the ABA Kentucky franchise that saw him average 3.7 points per game.

The six-foot-four Siegfried would hook up with Havlicek for seven seasons at Boston before moving on to other NBA teams for his final two years in the league. He would average 10.8 points per game.

With all that talent available, Knight became odd man out. Relegated to the bench, he was bitterly disappointed about his limited role. He had not expected to be a backup at Ohio State, and the reality was hard for him to take. He lobbied nonstop with Taylor for more playing time but the coach used him sparingly over the next three years.

Knight was, by the coach's view, a liability on defense—an irony given that industrial-strength pressuring defense became the trademark of the teams that Knight would later coach. But Taylor marked him as a step slow, which in the pressure defense the Buckeyes played was unforgivable.

"Certainly," said Taylor, "one of the reasons Bobby as a coach has always stressed and worked so hard on defense is that it was definitely one of his shortcomings as a player, and he knew it. Bobby's first idea of [coaching] defense is that of denying an opponent the ball, or contesting it. I suppose it might have come from what we did. We were the first in our league to pick up an opponent at mid-court and extend the passing lanes. That's one of Knight's principles."

Said Havlicek: "He just wasn't an individual who could jump over the rim and snatch rebounds, or put the stops to a guy. He worked hard at it [defense] but he always seemed to end up fouling someone."

Slow afoot or not, in his mind Knight felt he was good enough to play, and he refused to accept his backup role. He kept at Taylor, pushing for a chance to play, sometimes with an uncompromising attitude that, legend has it, prompted the coach to call him "The Brat from Orrville."

In later years, Taylor would deny hanging that tag on Knight, with whom he became close once Knight turned to coaching. But Taylor would acknowledge that during his varsity career Knight bitched and pouted, refusing to accept his substitute's role.

"Bobby hated not playing," said Taylor.

"Which is exactly what you want. You wants kids who want to compete, and that's just what Bobby was. But he was very blunt about thinking he should play more, and there were times when that was difficult for me and for him.

"He probably set the NCAA record for the number of times to quit a squad. He was all-world at Orrville, so he had an adjustment to make in college. He was a nonconformist, and that only made it harder for him."

No one questioned Knight's ability to shoot the ball—that low-trajectory jumper—or his court smarts, but on a team that boasted overall quickness Knight was never an easy fit. As Nowell would recall: "The chemistry was far better with, say, Richie Hoyt than with Bobby. Richie didn't dominate the ball. Bobby Knight couldn't drive. He wasn't quick enough. Wasn't a great dribbler. He could only shoot the jumper, and it had to be from far out—what would now be a college three-point shot. It wasn't a shot most coaches then would call a good shot."

What made his situation even more trying was the passion he had for the game. As Lucas recalled: "I remember that Bobby Knight was more interested in basketball than anyone on our team. He was a real student of the game and he analyzed what was going on all the time. He was so intense and wanted to play so bad that he was probably more critical of Coach Taylor than anyone else when he didn't play. He was very much a fighter back then, with spunk to the nth degree."

These were glory years for Ohio State, which from 1960 to 62 would win 78 of 84 games, capture three Big Ten titles, win the NCAA championship by beating California in Knight's sophomore year and then to lose to Cincinnati and Oscar Robertson in the NCAA finals the next two years. But Knight rarely shared in the good times.

The most points he scored as a Buckeye varsity player were the 15 he had against Delaware in his sophomore year. But in his three seasons, he rarely got off the bench long enough to have an impact on ball games. In Ohio State's NCAA championship victory, Knight got into the game only long enough to register a foul, no points. He would average 3.7 points per game as a sophomore, 4.4 points per game as a junior and 3.2 points per game as a senior.

Senior year was particularly hard to bear. He had gone into the season given a chance to be a starter at forward, opposite Havlicek. But once again he could not overcome his weakness as a defender, and, as in previous years, he was back on the pine.

According to Nowell: "A junior named Doug McDonald took his spot. And again Doug made the chemistry of the team better than Knight did. It's ironic. Bobby would do as a coach what he couldn't or wouldn't as a player. His Hoosiers pass to the open man. In reality he wasn't good at that, in contrast to other players on our team who had no trouble giving it up. His Indiana teams played hard and effective defense. Which he couldn't do as a player.

"Through the years at Ohio State it was very frustrating for Bobby. And you could see it . . . particularly in practices. He would get very physical in scrimmages. And guys would say to coach: 'Hey, get him off me,' or 'Hey, have him check somebody else.'

"Then there was a drill we did to get ready for road games, where things would be tougher and you wouldn't get the calls from the officials. The drill was called 'Bull in the ring.' You'd give one of the guys the ball, and the others would grab and poke at him and at the ball. Bobby was overaggressive. Players would complain."

While Knight, the player, was a negligible presence with the team, not so as a personality. On a team of crewcut midwestern boys, Knight at times could be a maverick spirit and more: a prankster, a cut-up, a guy who would keep the others laughing.

By today's standards, some of the antics appear fairly tame, Gearhart recalling: "The wildest thing we did was go to the movies on Saturday night and throw peanuts around. Lucas wouldn't go with us. Havlicek would, but once inside he'd move away."

In those days, his teammates knew Knight as "Dragon," a name said to have been conferred on him for the tall tale he told of his association with a fictitious motorcycle gang called The Dragons.

Knight was often center stage in those years when things got rowdy. As Frank Deford would note in a profile on Knight for *Sports Illustrated:*

> Dragon and a roommate led the Buckeyes in hustling tickets, and he stunned his wide-eyed teammates with his brash high jinks. On a trip to New York, he boldly swiped a couple of bottles of wine from Mama Leone's restaurant, and not only pilfered a few ties from a midtown shop, but with the contraband under his coat, he went over to a cop who entered the store at that moment and started chatting him up.

But even at Ohio State, Knight could flash a darker side. "He was," said Nowell, "a mixture of personalities. Like he is today. He could be smooth and enjoyable if he chose to. He had a quick wit. He was bright. But he could turn and be upset and angry. At our senior banquet . . . now I didn't hear it but the other fellows told me he said some things to [another player] that were inappropriate. He verbally ripped [him] as he has done to others over the years. Later, when he realized he was going into coaching, he made amends. It was frustration. It's why Bobby Knight liked the spotlight later and would do things to have it on him. It was funny to watch. The Indiana players would go through all the hard work of a game, and Bobby would dominate the scene. To my thinking, it came from the frustration of the years at Ohio State."

During his career at Ohio State, the Buckeye media guides for basketball would advise readers that Bobby Knight harbored a desire to coach in the future. That gibed with a school-assignment autobiography Knight had written at Orrville High in which he had projected himself as a basketball coach.

When Knight graduated in 1962 with a B.S in education—he majored in history and government—he flirted with the idea of studying law but decided against it. Offered the chance to be head basketball coach and an assistant football coach in Celina, Ohio, he turned it down for fear of being diverted by the football assignment from his real objective—to coach basketball.

Instead he accepted a job as an assistant basketball coach at Cuyahoga Falls (Ohio) High School, under Harold Andreas. Remembered Andreas: "I'm sure that when Bob went to Ohio State there was no doubt in his mind that he was going to be a regular. Then he had a disappointing experience there, and I think that made him want to prove something. Several of his teammates went on to play pro ball, so he had to do something to compensate. I really think he felt he had to prove he could be just as successful in basketball as his teammates.

"He was knowledgeable about the game and he was an outstanding competitor in college; Bob certainly came out of a highly successful team. I got to know him a bit before I hired him because one of the boys I coached in high school also played with OSU."

At Cuyahoga Falls, Andreas would get to know Knight better—as the fire-breathing, demanding coach of the Cuyahoga Falls junior varsity and an assistant with the varsity. When the junior varsity team lost its first game on a last-second shot, Knight ran a grueling, protracted practice the next day.

"You're going to kill these kids," Andreas told him. "You've got to let them go sometime."

"I agree," said Knight. "But it's going to be awhile."

The workout lasted for six hours and led to players' parents phoning to complain. But Knight remained Knight—the driven coach. At Cuyahoga Falls, he instituted a drill in which he would roll the ball onto the floor and have two players dive for it, his objective being to inculcate a disregard for floor burns and an instinctive hunger for ball possession.

In another drill, he would have a defender set up under the basket and then order a dribbler to take it full-tilt to the basket. The idea was for the man on defense to brace himself for the contact and draw the charging foul. He meant to have players who would give up their bodies to gain an advantage.

"He exhibited very early that intense competitiveness," said Andreas. "He had the same no-fooling philosophy of basketball he later would. Bob knew what had to be done with a team. He worked hard and got results.

"In those days it was popular for coaches to carry clipboards, and when things didn't go quite right with the jayvees, Bob slammed his clipboard to the floor and broke it. Before he left Cuyahoga Falls, I guess he set the record for broken clipboards."

6

Coaching Army

At the end of the year at Cuyahoga Falls, Knight considered attending law school at UCLA and working as a part-time assistant to the Bruins' head coach, John Wooden. But through Fred Taylor an opportunity arose for Knight to become an assistant coach at Army if he were willing to enlist immediately. The plan was for Knight to take basic training at Ft. Leonard Wood, Missouri—which he did—and then be assigned to coaching duties at the United States Military Academy.

A potential hitch developed when George Hunter, the Army coach with whom Knight had this understanding, was fired while Knight was undergoing basic training. But Hunter's successor, Tates Locke, agreed to honor Hunter's commitment. Pfc. Knight would coach the Army plebes and assist Locke with the varsity.

Locke, who had played his college ball at Ohio Wesleyan, and Knight were soulmates—two men crazy for basketball—at a school where football was the priority.

"We were both young guys," Locke later recalled. "Army was my first head coaching job, and was Bobby's first college coaching job. I've never been able to work any closer with anybody in my life. You hear all of these war stories about guys recruiting on a shoestring and living out of the back of a car. We had a $500 budget at Army and we recruited the whole United States on it. That and two Army cars. We drove everywhere, did everything out of a car, did anything to save money.

"We wrote every high school in the country and we didn't have a secretary then. Bobby and I banged away on a typewriter. You could look in his office and there were newspapers from all over the country stacked up, four or five months behind. Bobby would have the team manager take the sports sections out of them, and he would read every one of them.

"He was more than just an assistant to me. He was a friend. We did everything together. We played intramural ball at Army, and both almost got Article 15s for starting a fight in one of those leagues which played at noon.

"We would play one-on-one against each other. I remember one day we were going to play American University in Washington. We had a team workout and when we got through we told the kids to go and shower. An hour and a half later we were still going after each other one-on-one and the kids were standing around watching."

The two men coached with the same sort of single-mindedness, both of them volatile presences on the bench.

"Bobby was a good player, a lot better player than I was," said Locke. "But I think a lot of his success as a coach would come from not being as great a player as he wanted to be. He used to be really fiery during games. The two of us on the bench looked like a Chinese fire drill.

"We were playing Washington State in '64–65 and the officials were giving us a bad time in the first half. Bobby and I had gotten two technicals on the bench in the first half. Then, when we went into the locker-room at halftime, I noticed he wasn't there but I figured he would be along in a few minutes.

"Well, he came in and said he had something to tell me. I told him to let it wait because first we needed to work out how we were going to get the opening tip in the second half. He had his head hanging down, the way he always does when he feels bad, and said there was no need to worry about getting the tip at the start of the half because he had followed the officials off the floor at halftime and had gotten a technical and we would start the half with that.

"He said he had something else to tell me. I said it could wait, but he said he had to tell me right then. He said he was going to have to sit in the stands the second half 'cause he'd gotten booted. About that time a Pinkerton guard showed up and escorted him into the stands."

Locke guided Army teams to winning seasons in '63–64 and '64–65 before accepting the head coach's job at Miami of Ohio. That left Army without a basketball coach. On a whim, the 24-year-old Knight inquired about the vacant position—and got it.

In 1964, Knight had married an Orrville girl, Nancy Lou Falk, whom he'd known since the fifth grade, For his first two months as head coach, with Nancy and young son Tim to support, Knight earned only $99 a month because he was still an enlisted man. But when he mustered out, his salary was upgraded to civilian standards.

While Knight would be handicapped at Army

by the academy's height restriction—cadets could be no taller than six-foot-six—and by the ordinary basketball talent the school drew, he made do. His system was unswervingly basic—an offense that relied on picks and cuts and probing, multiple passes to create a high-percentage shot and a defense in which players applied pressure, denying the pass and doubling the ball. It was Bobby Knight Basketball 101—a disciplined, fundamentally sound game that required intelligence, high energy and laser focus by his players. It hadn't margin for free-wheeling types, partial to run and gun. Knight's type of ballplayer would be the quintessential gym rat and overachiever, a kid who had more heart than talent.

The Knight who coached Army was no less demanding, or shrill, than he had been at Cuyahoga Falls, or would be at Indiana. Knight was not an evolved species. He came to the coaching business fully formed as a man who worked his players unrelentingly, a coach who snarled, insisted, persisted, cursed, shouted, denigrated, all in the cause of victory.

Players adapted to Knight, or sat. For instance, Mike Krzyzewski. The future Coach K of Duke University had been a scorer at Weber High in Chicago—a player who had a virtual green light to shoot the ball. But Knight decided what he needed from Krzyzewski—what would make the team better—was Krzyzewski reconstituted as a tenacious defender and playmaker.

"I was quick to see Mike could play on our team, but none of it related to what he did in high school," Knight said. "We had better shooters than him. But in becoming the kind of player we wanted him to be, Mike gained an appreciation for basketball that a scorer never could. He was the best I ever had at saying, 'Hey, I'm just an average player, so I've got to play my ass off.' "

Krzyzewski was a three-year letterman at Army and, as a senior, captained Knight's '68–69 team. In three seasons at West Point, this former high-school hotshot would average only 6.2 points per game in 69 games, but he would provide the elements Knight needed to create a winner. And for Knight that was all that mattered.

"At West Point, I made up my mind to win—GOTTA win," said Knight. "Not at all costs. Never that. But winning was the hub of everything I was doing. And understand, I've never gotten over West Point."

It was not easy duty for the players. Imagine what it must have been like for those cadets. Days that began at 10 minutes to six and were full of the rigors of military discipline. As Knight put it: "They are REQUIRED to go to class. They march to lunch; they march to dinner. Chin in. Chest out. Gut in. All day."

Then it's four o'clock and time for basketball—a boy's game that offers the prospect of fun. Fun. A break in the rigid routine. A chance to breath. But there's coach Knight, with his Darth Vader menace, and if you're Cadet Mike Silliman or Bill Schutsky or Jim Oxley or Krzyzewski, it's no late-breaking news that the practice you're about to undergo will be as much fun as a dentist's drill applied to a quaking molar without novacaine.

But that was the deal, and would be for Knight's players over the next 30-odd years. It was a rite of passage. Bear up under Coach's badgering, ignore the insults, the profanity, the assaults on your manhood, and there was a chance that you'd emerge with a keener insight into the game—and a heightened talent. Put up with all the bullshit and give the man your best, and the deal was sealed. From the day you left Cuyahoga Falls/West Point/ Indiana, coach Knight was looking out for you.

As Tom Miller, a former Army center, would say: "If you paid the price and worked to your fullest potential, you can count on Bob Knight for the rest of your life. He takes a personal interest in his players on and off the court.

"One of the players at Army injured his eye before graduation, and because you had to meet all the physical requirements for military service, that player was in jeopardy of being discharged. But Coach intervened, and the school allowed this senior to graduate."

When Krzyzewski's father, Bill, died during Mike's senior year, Knight turned the team over to his assistants , then missed three days of practice so that he could fly to Chicago with the player, attend the funeral and then comfort Krzyzewski and his mother, Emily. Krzyzewski had given Knight his all, and Knight now reciprocated. The gesture touched Krzyzewski because of what it meant to his mother. "Coach just sat around the kitchen for hours, telling her stories, keeping her mind occupied," said Krzyzewski. "It was as if nothing else mattered to him right then other than helping my mom and me."

In the 70s, when Knight left Army for Indiana, the West Point basketball program tanked. Things hit rock-bottom in the 1973–74 season when Army went 3–22. The coaching job became vacant. One hundred and twenty people applied for it. But Army hired the man Bobby Knight recommended, his then-assistant coach at I-U, Mike Krzyzewski.

With the limited talent he had at Army, Knight's approach—the patient offense, the aggressive defense—tended to produce low-scoring and often closely contested games—games that were, as Knight joked, "about as exciting as watching wet paint dry." But, as Knight recalled, "Our talent was such that a single bad call could beat us, so I wasn't about to let two guys with whistles take away what we worked so hard to achieve."

Knight worked the refs.

"When I started out at Army it was always a battle between me and the officials," he said. "I guess it was because our kids were so small and worked so hard that when some official blew one—and they are human—I went nuts. It's hard to sit still when you see your 6'1" kid beat some 6'9" guy and then get called for something he didn't do."

Quickly Knight acquired a reputation for not only harping at the officials but, when not getting his way, going off like a July 4th cherry bomb. He hollered, he cursed, he knocked over water coolers. But the incident that marked Knight indelibly occurred during his first season as the Cadets' head coach, in '65–66. Army was playing Boston College in the ECAC Holiday Festival at

Madison Square Garden when an official's call provoked Knight. He stomped the first thing he saw, which happened to be a wooden folding chair that sat next to the Garden's timekeeper, Feets Broudy. The chair was smashed beyond repair, and Knight drew the first of the many technicals he would incur over his six seasons as coach of Army. Soon enough, the New York press had tagged him "Bobby T," the T standing for technical foul.

There would be other outbursts during his six years as Army's coach. He once broke a finger when he drove his fist into a wall following a discussion with Army's athletic director. He destroyed an entire set of golf clubs during one particularly poor round. He kicked a waste basket that stopped at the feet of two Army generals.

But the chair-smashing incident established his image as a hothead. It was played up big in the nation's press, inciting exaggerated flourishes. One Chicago writer had Knight throwing the chair into the stands, another scribe said he threw one of his players after the chair. Whatever. Knight viewed the press's coverage of him then and later as perpetually misdirected, even when it was an objective reflection of his misbehavior. There was something of a kill-the-messenger attitude the coach bore the press.

"Some of those New York writers," he would say, "would assassinate Helen Keller. I kicked one chair and I was marked for life."

In fact, Knight may have gotten off easy. In later years, Bob Cousy, the NBA great, would tell of the time he was coaching Boston College against Army and saw an angry Knight with his hand against a player's throat as he backed the cadet against the arena corridor wall at halftime.

His temperament would not have been so publicized had Army been a loser. But Knight's Cadet teams were a revelation, managing not only to compete against taller, more naturally gifted squads but consistently beating them. As Don DeVoe, an assistant coach to Knight, put it: "Knight was taking physically spent kids and getting more out of them than the coaches whose kids slept until noon."

And Army did it Knight's way—a patient offense and his trademark stingy defense.

"Basketball is the most simple game in the world," said Knight. "You work to get good shots and you limit your opponent's good ones and you win the game. Nothing very complex about that."

In six years under Knight Army won 102 games and lost 50; beat Navy all six years; had the most victories for an Army team (22); played in four National Invitational tournaments; had a team defense that three times led the nation.

In Knight's defensive system each defender had three obligations: (1) not let his man get the ball; (2) When he does get it, not to let him do what he wants with it; and (3) If he takes a shot or passes it, not to let him get it back.

Knight preached being aware every moment of where the ball was and being in position to stop it. While Army teams played man to man, they were taught to work as a unit—to switch when necessary and to double-team. It was not simply a matter of keeping an eye on your man.

In Knight's first season, the Cadets ranked eighth nationally in defense, allowing an average of 62.9 points a game. The next year they were third with 57.4. Then came three consecutive seasons in which they were number one, with 57.9, 53.5 and 54.1.

It was hard-nosed basketball, and Knight took pride in his guys' hell-for-leather attitude, recalling, for instance, his six foot five center, Mike Gyovai:

"We went to Wyoming where they had a 6'9" center. Going up for a rebound, Mike busted the guy in the mouth with his elbow. Blood spurted everywhere. I can see it now as plain as the day it happened. The 6'9" guy is standing there, holding his hand over his mouth, wondering if he's got any teeth left. There's blood all over Mike, too. So Mike wipes the blood off his shoulder and then wipes his hand off on the 6'9" guy's shirt and then trots away, leaving the guy counting his teeth."

Through his first five seasons at the Point, Knight's teams had records of 18–8, 13–8, 20–5, 18–10 and 22–6.

"I've never seen a period in my lifetime at the academy when the student body was so buoyed by a team," said Major General Ray Murphy, Army's athletic director. "You talk about esprit— the basketball team brought it on, but it was fortunately the corps that was pushing the basketball team. . . . Magnficent."

For Knight, the feeling was mutual.

"I really enjoyed West Point," Knight would say years later. "There was a strong discipline approach to things, and it was a very, very good atmosphere for me personally because we were able to have a very tough approach to things.

"To be successful at West Point, I found I had to be a little bit tougher than anybody else. I've always found that when you let up on somebody, it's like putting a hole in a damn; pretty soon things get out of control. But I ran into conflicts with that approach. Even people at West Point would say, 'He's too tough on the cadets.' But why the hell shouldn't we be? I mean, you're watching Army playing in Madison Square Garden, you ought to think these guys are going to be able to get out and protect the country, too. That was my approach to it."

Knight was a perfect fit for West Point and its tradition of discipline. Years later, he would write: "My first feeling of the strength and character possessed both by the Cadets and those teaching at the Academy occurred only minutes after I had driven through the main entrance at Thayer Gate and parked at the physical education building. I entered the building through a door over which was inscribed, 'Upon the fields of friendly strife are sown the seeds that on other fields on other days will bear the fruit of victory.' I was a history major and I had read enough to know that Douglas MacArthur had made this statement when discussing the value and benefit of athletic competition as it would relate to later life. I was awed and it was a feeling I had many times during my years there.

"The basic foundation of military structure is discipline. My years at West Point allowed me to develop not only an appreciation of discipline but also find a way discipline could be applied to basketball and to the players I would coach."

As an avid reader of history, Knight had a more than passing knowledge of military affairs, which he drew on as a coach. *The Art of War,* written 500 years before Christ by the Chinese warrior Sun-Tzu, was compatible with Knight's ideas about eliciting the strongest effort from his players. In fact, he would quote from Sun-Tzu's work to show the parallels between warfare and coaching basketball.

Like this passage: "Regard your soldiers as your children and they will follow you wherever you lead. Look upon them as your beloved sons and they will stand by you even unto death. If, however, you are indulgent, unable to make your authority felt, kindhearted but unable to enforce your commands, then your soldiers must be likened to spoiled children. They are useless for all practical purposes."

At a time when the Vietnam war was polarizing the country, when a youth culture espoused sex, drugs and rock and roll, Bobby Knight's short-haired boys were the antithesis of all that. At a time when the college game's marquee attraction, Pistol Pete Maravich of LSU, shot the ball with impunity—40, 50 times a game—and played little defense, Knight's Army teams were out of a 1950s time capsule. They played a purist's basketball, a team-oriented game. They had the fresh-scrubbed perspective of Chip Hilton clones.

Ah, Chip. As a boy growing up in Orrville, Knight had relished those Hilton novels and admired their author, Clair Bee. But it was while at Army that Knight would get to know, and befriend, Bee in his other role—as a longtime, highly-regarded college basketball coach.

At Orrville, Knight had been close to his coaches, Shunkwiler and Graham, older men whose counsel, and friendship, he valued. It was, it turned out, a lifetime habit. Bee would be one of many older, established coaches that Knight as coach sought out while at West Point. Bee, Joe Lapchick, Pete Newell, Hank Iba and Red Auerbach—they became mentors with whom Knight explored Xs and Os. They were his Yodas, and he treated them—uncharacteristically for this socially pugnacious coach—with deference.

"Clair Bee and I were really close," said Knight. "We were damn near like father and son."

In his time, Bee was an innovator who formulated the 1–3—zone and knew great success as coach at Rider College and then Long Island University—a winning percentage of 82.7 percent.

"Mr. Bee," said Knight, "seemed to have an instantaneous recognition of what was going on. He was at New York Military Academy, and he would come to our scrimmages occasionally. I had him talk to the players one time and he went right through the room by their numbers. He didn't know their names. He told one player, 'You didn't block out.' He told another, 'When you were shooting free throws, you were looking at the floor instead of the bucket.' He was amazing. I talked to him endlessly about preparing for the season, about preparing for a game. He taught me tactics, especially the manipulation of the offense."

Through the years, Knight would communicate regularly with Bee, in person or by phone. Bee was his confidante, his advisor, his friend.

"I got to know Bob when he was at Army," said Bee. "I watched this young kid who had so much on the ball, so dedicated, so serious. I never saw him smile. He asked me to come and watch his games. Afterward, we'd go out and talk. He'd have coffee and I'd drink beer.

"I don't want to step in for any credit, though. So help me god, this kid would make good if he didn't know anyone. He lives this game. When you are dedicated and willing to listen to someone who has been knocked around and been around, how can you help but succeed."

When Knight's Army team lost a last-second heartbreaker to St. John's, 60–59, in the semifinals of the 1970 National Invitation Tournament, Knight was, as he recalled, "emotionally whipped."

"I went to the press room," he said, "and I couldn't talk."

At 9 o'clock that night, he called Bee to vent his hurt. Minutes after they hung up, Bee wrote him a letter that said in part:

> It was a heartbreaker and probably your last big test in the crucible of fire that molds a man into a man. . . .
> Disappointment and heartbreaks always strengthen a man. Your day will come, this I know. Your dedication, determination, desire and devotion to the game will carry you to new heights. I hope I am around to cheer for you and your team when that day comes.

The new heights to which Bee alluded were about to be breeched—in the basketball hotbed of Indiana. It was 1971, and Bobby Knight—after his only losing season as a coach, at Army—was moving on.

7

Hoosier Hysteria

Basketball was more than a sport in Indiana. It was a grass-roots tradition, steeped in history.

Amid Indiana's farflung rural hamlets, basketball offered a social opportunity—a chance for folks from communities separated by mere mileage to come together over a game.

No state had embraced basketball on the high school level as Indiana had. Commencing in 1911, its all-comers state tournament enabled schools with a couple dozen able-bodied youths to go up against the powerhouses from large industrial cities that could draw from a talent pool of thousands.

From 1928, tournament title games were played in 14,000-seat Butler Arena, at the time the biggest gym in the world. Dr. James Naismith, who had invented the game for his phys-ed students in 1891 in Springfield, Massachusetts, saw the crowd that filled the place and became goggle-eyed. He said that basketball might have been invented in Massachusetts, but Indiana was where it grew up.

Indeed, the backyard hoop-and-backboard became a fixture throughout the state, and the fascination with the game was obsessive. It was reflected in the proliferation of large-sized gyms that exceeded many a small town's population and yet managed to end up packed to the rafters as fans drove in from surrounding burgs. "Hoosier Hysteria" was how the natives referred to the annual boys high school tournament.

When Bob (Slick) Leonard, who starred at Indiana and later in the NBA, graduated from high school in 1950, 714 teams vied for the title. "Sometimes," said Leonard, "there were only 12 to 15 boys in the whole school, but they all played. Every town had a team. And if that team advanced to regionals in Martinsville—that's where John Wooden is from, you know—the town locked up."

Hoosier Hysteria reached a peak in 1954 when tiny Milan High School upset big-city Muncie Central as young Bobby Plump nailed the game-winning jumper at the final buzzer. That victory took on mythic proportions throughout Indiana in the years that followed and became celebrated by Hollywood in the 1986 film *Hoosiers,* starring Gene Hackman—a thinly veiled version of real events.

No surprise that a state so invested in the game had generated its share of basketball greats: Wooden, Leonard, Larry Bird, Oscar Robertson, George McGinnis, Shawn Kemp, Dick Barnett, Tom and Dick Van Arsdale.

Wooden, who would win a record 10 NCAA titles as coach of UCLA, recalled that his first basketball was created by his mother, who filled a black sock with rags.

"My dad tacked up on the barn a tomato basket for a goal," said Wooden. "Not a peach basket like Dr. Naismith. We grew tomatoes."

The grass-roots fervor for the game carried over to the college level, where a coach named Branch McCracken had made the state university, in Bloomington, a fan favorite. McCracken, who coached Indiana University from 1939 to 1943 and from 1947 to 1965, produced run-and-gun teams, nicknamed the "Hurrying Hoosiers," that routinely had winning records—and twice, in 1940 and 1953, were NCAA champions.

But by the late 60s, Hoosier teams suffered through sub-.500 campaigns and when the

1970–71 season saw a player rebellion under coach Lou Watson, the athletic administration at I-U decided enough was enough—it was time for a change. Enter Bobby Knight.

No brass bands celebrated Knight's arrival. To the contrary, the 30-year-old coach, who signed on for a five-year hitch at I-U, was widely thought to be out of his element—his slow-down game an affront to a team that historically played the racehorse game.

On April 1, 1971, Knight's first day on the job at Indiana, a *New York Times* story quoted an anonymous "Indiana expert" as saying: "Knight will never make it here. We run, shoot and gamble."

Well, times were about to change. Bobby Knight had no intention of being cowed by precedents. The game would be played his way, which meant defense and a slow patient offense calculated to get good shots. And Bobby Knight would be the first and last word on I-U basketball. Once, on passing a sign that read "HURRYING HOOSIERS," he said, "The guy that wrote that must be the world's greatest optimist."

In his office at the spanking new Assembly Hall, a $13.9-million facility with a seating capacity of 17,000, there were pretty fair clues that Knight was a man who would do things his way and brook no interference.

On the walls of his office hung this sign:

> By your own soul, learn to live.
> And if a man thwart you, pay no heed.
> If a man hate you, have no care.
> Sing your song, dream your dream.
> Pray your prayer.
> By your own soul, learn to live.

There was also a wall hanging with the words of General George S. Patton Jr., a hero of Knight's:

> You have to be single-minded,
> Drive only one thing on which you have decided,
> And if it look as if you might be getting there,
> All kinds of people, including some you thought were your loyal friends,
> Will suddenly show up doing their hypocritical God damnest to trip you, blacken you,
> And break your spirit.

The quotations provided a clue to Knight's hard-edged personality. He was not a man who camouflaged his feelings, or blunted his words. With Knight, any occasion might provoke him to test you. Conversation was an aggressive act, a challenge, Knight probing to find out who you were.

"I don't like people very well because most of them lack intestinal fortitude or integrity," he said. "People cannot, for the most part, tolerate someone who tells them to go get screwed."

In his first season at Indiana, when the team suffered a five-game losing streak and an influential Hoosier alumnus chided the coach at a social gathering for playing "that damn dull basketball," Knight told him, "If you don't like the way we play, then stay away from the games."

The alumnus told Knight he was a big contributor to I-U athletics and in fact gave $100,000 to Hoosier programs.

Retorted Knight, in a voice audible to the entire gathering, "Fuck your contributions. Whatever you give to the university, I'll double."

Later, he would joke: "I think all alumni should be canonized. That way the coach would only have to kiss their rings."

But make no mistake. Bobby Knight was in charge, and he let you know it. Steve Downing was a junior at I-U when Knight took over. The first time he met the coach, Downing held out his hand, but Knight refused to shake it. Looking him straight in the eye, he warned Downing: "I'm going to tell you something, you're not going to play here! You don't want to play defense!"

At the team's first practice, former I-U grads accustomed to watching the squad's workouts discovered that their presence was no longer welcome. Like the Gene Hackman coach in *Hoosiers,* Knight booted them out. His practices would be closed so there would be no distractions. In the years that followed, the court would be curtained off when the team practiced, and rare were the visitors given permission to watch.

For the players, the practices were perpetual hell. Preseason conditioning drills—sprints that were topped by running the 109 steps to the last row of the new arena—left them numbed and glassy-eyed. Knight would catch their outraged expressions and say, "Your being tired is the least of my concerns. I don't care."

Once practice began officially, the Hoosiers were introduced to those "suicide drills" that Knight had used before, at Cuyahoga Falls and at West Point. Pretty soon, the players were generating floor burns as they dove, competitively, for loose balls.

"You learn in a hurry that the ball is golden," said Steve Green, a six-foot-seven freshman.

"When I saw that fumble drill just coming out of high school, I thought, 'Oh, God.' Now in a game you just dive for a ball without thinking."

Another drill Knight used had the team manager toss a ball against the backboard and then watch three players scramble for the rebound. The player who came down with the ball was then obliged to take it hard to the hoop while the two defenders challenged him vigorously.

"It's an old Ohio State drill," Knight said. "A lot of hacking and fouling. Havlicek put seven stitches in my eyebrow during one of those things. They sewed me up on the training table and I finished the practice. You didn't get a lot of sympathy there either."

What the players got was Coach's unrelenting pressure, administered with his characteristic corrosive language. Knight used intimidation and fear. He rode his players mercilessly, on the premise that if they could get through his torture the games would come easy to them.

"Very few of us," said Knight, "reach our full potential. There's a helluva crowd at the bottom of the ladder and you've got to work through that crowd. Human nature is that thing that prevents us from reaching our potential. It's human nature to be satisfied with a C instead of trying for a B, or for being an 85 percent free throw shooter instead of a 90 percent shooter. Try to beat human nature. That's your opponent in everything you do.

"Most people—at the core of their personality—have a great fear of not being liked, and they subvert, bend or disregard their ideas and principles when they teach. A parent who doesn't want to irritate a daughter or son might do that, and I think that's the worst thing that can be done.

"I, fortunately have never worried about irritating people. I don't think you can teach and be worried about irritating people. The learning experience is best accomplished by being motivated, and a motivator isn't always a guy who pats you on the ass. He's the guy who kicks you in the ass occasionally."

That was the working theory, and it wasn't—as Knight himself would concede—for everybody:

"I'll see a kid play and I say to myself, 'That kid can't play for me.' Well, that simply means one thing—the kid can't play for me. . . . That doesn't mean that he's a bad player or that he's a bad kid. He may be a hell of a player and he may be the best kid possible, but he has a way of playing or an approach to playing that isn't going to fit into what I want to do. Then, I also have to think to myself that it isn't just that that kid can't play for me, but from that kid's standpoint, I'm not the coach for him.

"I can't take a mediocre athlete and make him a great basketball player. And I can't take a kid who's a pain in the ass and make him the nicest kid in the world. But if you have players with average talent and excellent character, you have a chance of being a better team than with the reverse combination.

"The type of player we look for is first of all a good person with good character traits because that's the kind of person who becomes an unselfish and team-oriented basketball player. The physical attributes we want are quickness and wiry strength. And he must have an intelligence for the game. I always say that the mental aspect in basketball is to physical as four is to one."

For Indiana players, a good part of the mental game was in learning how to deal with Coach's temperament, in practice and during games. Following a 52–51 heartbreaking loss to Minnesota on January 8, 1971, Hoosier guard Dave Shepherd recalled that Knight went bonkers and "dismantled the locker room pretty good, throwing benches and stuff."

On the bus ride to the airport, no one dared sit within 10 rows of Knight.

The paradox of Knight was that for all his

fury, for all the over-the-top behavior, he was a man who, in a business of pragmatists and sleazy opportunists, had standards. He insisted his players go to class and get their degrees. He refused to cut corners in recruiting—there would be no under-the-table deals to bring a hot-shot high school kid to Bloomington. Knight offered his hell-bent Basketball 101 and a chance to get an education. Nothing more.

And as he had made it plain to rich alumni, and basketball-crazy I-U grads, that things would be done his way, so too did he educate Hoosier fans. Knight might be obsessed with winning, but it had to be victory wrought the right way. He did not want Assembly Hall to become a "snake pit"—an environment in which visiting teams were assailed by crude chants or thrown objects. When unsavory incidents occurred early on, Knight would step to the public-address announcer's table and, microphone in hand, tell the crowd to cease-and-desist, goddammit—and threaten to ask the game officials to nail I-U with a technical foul, or even forfeit, if misbehavior wasn't immediately corrected.

Once during a Notre Dame game, when a fan hurled a paper cup toward the floor and hit the Irish's John Shumate near his eye with a piece of ice, the public address announcer's mild rebuke to the crowd about good sportsmanship was interrupted by Knight, who grabbed the microphone and said, "The next time some stupid fuck throws anything on the floor, the home team will forfeit the fucking game."

Conversely, on another occasion when the crowd didn't rise to the level of support Knight felt appropriate, he was back at that microphone, telling the fans to "get off your dead asses."

From the outset, Bobby Knight made it plain to all concerned that it was his show and you got to tag along only if you adhered to his terms. But Knight's way worked. The floundering Indiana basketball program righted itself under the coach. I-U overcame its five-game losing streak in Knight's first year and ended up with a 17–7 record, as attendance more than doubled. A year later, in 1972–73, the 22–6 Hoosiers won the Big Ten title and, in the NCAA tournament, beat Marquette and Kentucky before succumbing to Bill Walton and eventual-champion UCLA, 70–59.

Pleased with the job that Knight had done, I-U renegotiated Knight's deal to extend for five more seasons at a reported $28,500 per year.

8

"We'll Be Back"

By 1973–74, Knight had the makings of a special team. He had begun to assemble a group of young players that not only had talent but, it would turn out, shared a rare chemistry too. On the best teams the sum is greater than its parts—players intuit one another and instinctively fulfill roles that serve the greater good. At Indiana, that might mean steering dribblers into traps when on defense and on offense exploiting the impatience of opposition defenders with savvy cuts and pinpoint passing.

Knight had players who, time would show, had that gift for team play. In 1973–74, even as these young turks flashed promise, they were still learning. The Indiana team would go 23–5 and win the Big Ten title again, but Knight's core group of four sophomores—Scott May, Tom Abernethy, Bobby Wilkerson, Quinn Buckner and a six-ten freshman center named Kent Benson—would only get better.

Benson, a polite redhead who was from New Castle, Indiana, was a work-in-progress. He was a big strong lad whose prodigious appetite—he had once demolished 33 pieces of barbecued chicken, along with five dishes of cake and ice cream and 11 soft drinks, at one sitting—was not matched by his hunger for Knight-intense defense. Or by a hunger even for the game. As a freshman, Benson had enraged Knight when, returning from Christmas vacation, he told the coach he had not touched a basketball for three whole days.

The coach's angry reaction brought a focus to Benson's outlook that had been missing. "Right then and there, that's when I really grew up," said Benson.

For all his height, Benson was not a gifted jumper. But he made do by using his upper body strength to block out opponents and get position for rebounds. He had deceptive quickness around the basket, moving well without the ball. That movement often shook him loose for routine lay-ups in I-U's motion offense.

May was a six-foot-seven forward from Sandusky, Ohio, who roamed the floor with a silky ease. He was as skilled a pure shooter—deadly from 15 feet—as I-U had, and worked hard on defense and the boards. He had also overcome a tendency to drop passes when he joined the Hoosier squad, a flaw that inspired teammate Buckner to jokingly call him "Stonehands."

The six-foot-seven Abernethy was, in Knight's term, "a sacrificer"—a player who was always performing the less celebrated acts of the game. Abernethy set picks, made judicious passes and hounded like a guard dog on defense even as he chipped in a few points here, a few points there.

Wilkerson was a spidery six-foot-seven guard whose elongated reach, quickness, and jumping ability—Knight had him jumping center—made him a troublesome defender. Defense was the objective Knight had given him, and Wilkerson applied himself with vigor against opposition guards.

Then there was the six-foot-three Buckner, who for his freshman and sophomore years had moonlighted as a defensive back for the I-U football team. But by 1974–75, when the young turks would become a force, Buckner had given up football to concentrate on basketball, much to the delight of Bobby Knight. Although Buckner was built like an armored personnel carrier, he had the speed and subtlety to lead the squad in steals. He was the team leader, and an enduring favorite of Knight's for his selfless attitude, his perpetual hustle.

In 1974–75, Benson, Buckner, Wilkerson and May would join six-foot-seven senior forward Steve Green as starters. Abernethy and a six-foot-six senior named John Laskowski, a.k.a "Super Sub for his ability to come off the bench and generate instant offense, would back up the starters.

As individuals, all seven would go on to have careers in pro basketball.

Green would play one season in the ABA with Utah and St. Louis and average 9.1 points per game, and then play three NBA seasons with Indiana and average 4.6 points per game.

Abernethy would play five seasons in the NBA, for Los Angeles, Golden State and Indiana, and average 5.6 points per game.

Laskowski would play two years for the Chicago Bulls and average 7.1 points per game.

Wilkerson would play seven seasons with Seattle, Denver, Chicago and Cleveland and average 10.1 points per game.

May would play seven seasons with Chicago, Milwaukee and Detroit and average 10.4 points per game.

Buckner would play ten seasons with Milwaukee, Boston and Indiana and average 8.2 points per game.

And Benson would play 11 seasons with Milwaukee, Detroit, Utah and Cleveland and average 9.1 points per game.

While none of the seven became big stars in the pro game, the fact that they had NBA careers is a measure of the serious talent that Knight had at hand. But it was a credit to the coach, and these players, that the seven young men would submit to Knight's system, subordinating their egos to function as a team.

And what a team Indiana was in '74–75. It lit up Assembly Hall those winter nights and created a Hoosier Hysteria all its own. On game days, fans—most of them wearing a red sweater, jacket or jersey—descended on Bloomington from as far away as Gary and Elkhart, Fort Wayne and Evansville. On the walkway leading up to the arena, scalpers would be hawking $4 general admission tickets for double and triple their face value, and courtside seats for as much as $40.

Inside the arena, as the school's all-girl Red Steppers put the final touches on a hip-shaking dance routine to the music of the I-U pep band, the sell-out crowd that included Indiana governor Otis Bowen arrived. Signs were posted over the arena walls, proclaiming fan support: "TO OUR COACHES AND TEAM, OUR ATTITUDE IS GRATITUDE." Punsters in the crowd announced their heroes with other signs: "KNIGHT TIME," "MAY DAY" and for reserve Jim Crews, "KEEP ON CREWSIN'."

As the Indiana team took the floor, the band stuck up "The Mighty Quinn," a tribute to Buckner, and the fans raised a din rivaling a jet at take-off while cheerleaders and pompom girls urged them on.

Then the game would begin. Knight, in his bright plaid jacket and loosened tie, prowled the sidelines watching his team disassemble the likes of Tennessee Tech, Kansas, Notre Dame, Texas A&M, Toledo, Creighton—the early-season opposition meant to toughen I-U for the Big Ten schedule that lay ahead.

But whatever team Indiana faced, it kept steamrollering its opponents. Sixteen, seventeen, eighteen straight games the Hoosiers had won by February, their average victory margin 27 points, the best in the country. The games were like clinics as the Hoosiers shot 52 percent from the floor. And when the Indiana defense held the foe to under 50 points, there was an added benefit for its fans. McDonald's outlets in Bloomington offered a free hamburger, french fries and soft drink to anyone with a ticket stub from the game. By season's end, a McDonald's spokesman would estimate that the Bloomington outlets had given away more than 18,000 hamburgers and french fries.

Playing Indiana, quipped Knight's former coach, Fred Taylor, was "like making love to a porcupine."

Success didn't spoil Bobby Knight.

He remained true to character—a man in search of controversy.

When the Downtown Service Club of Bloomington, a booster club, presented him with a seatbelt as a gag gift at a preseason luncheon—the belt a reminder of his tendency to explode off the bench and incur technical fouls—Knight was not amused. He lashed out at the crowd, which was comprised of his supporters, for their bad taste.

Then, on December 8, 1974, in the team's third game of the season, against Kentucky, Knight was stage center in another incident.

Late in the game, with I-U ahead by some 30 points, Knight got upset by an official's call. When he began jawing with the official, Kentucky coach Joe B. Hall needled him about overreacting.

That offended Knight, who told Hall, "You coach your end and I'll coach mine."

Hall then approached Knight at the scorer's table.

Said Knight: "I told him, 'Joe, I've been coaching this game for 10 years and I've never said a word to another coach about what he was doing.' He said what he had said was said in a good-natured way and I accepted it at that."

Then Knight tapped Hall on the side of the head. At least that's what Knight would later call it. A tap. Trouble was that a Hall assistant, Lynn Nance, saw it as being far more emphatic than a "tap." Viewing it as a hostile whack, Nance jumped up from the bench and yelled, "You son of a bitch, do that to me."

After order was restored and the game finished, Hall and Knight resumed talking at the scorer's table. Referee Chuck Allen and I-U athletic director Bill Orwig suggested they talk in private. Hall refused to walk off the floor with Knight.

In the press conference afterward, Knight said: "He [Hall] told me as far as he was concerned that was not a good-natured tap on the head. I had told him that was the way I had intended it. I honestly think anyone who has seen us play has seen me do the same thing to our kids many times as a show of affection. If he is upset about that I can understand it and I publicly apologize."

Hall was upset. He told reporters: "He personally humiliated me, and I'll never forget it."

Sometime later, as the incident fomented, Knight apparently had had enough of trying to appease the Wildcat coach.

"If I was really going to hit the sonuvabitch," he said, "I'd have knocked him into the third row."

A more serious problem arose on February 22 against Purdue. By now, Indiana's undefeated streak was at 25. But on this night, the Hoosiers would get unlucky. Oh, they would beat Purdue in a squeaker 83–82 for their 26th consecutive win, but it would be a costly victory. For late in the first half, as Scott May went up for a rebound, he felt a numbness when his left forearm made contact against bone of a Purdue player. When May advised Knight he was in pain, the coach removed him from the game with 2:24 remaining in the half. X-rays would determine that May had broken his radial, the largest bone in the forearm. With a cast on the damaged arm, May would return to play a few minutes in late-season games but he would not be the same player because of the injury.

Yet with or without May, the team remained a coach's dream. It mowed down the opposition, operating in so surehanded a way that even the usually pessimistic Knight sounded like a man who had found the miracle cure at Lourdes.

"It's a very interesting group to watch—even for me," said Knight. "Our whole operation is totally collective. There's no fiery individual getting the rest of the guys fired up. It's more like a board with everyone having an equal say. It's the closest I've come to a collective team in my coaching career."

That team would finish the regular season undefeated in 29 games, and look to underscore its brilliance with an NCAA title. But on the way to that ultimate glory, Joe B. Hall got revenge for Knight's so-called "tap."

On March 22, 1975, in the mid-East regional title game, Kentucky knocked Indiana out of the NCAA tournament and spoiled its perfect season by edging the Hoosiers 92–90.

I-U fans would say that had May been at full strength, no team in the country could have stopped this team. But the reality was that the dream season had been shattered. Bobby Knight's Hoosiers (31–1) had lost.

Afterward, the coach stood on a podium for 30 minutes, addressing the media. His voice was raspy, his eyes red. When he finished his comments, he put an arm around his dejected ten-year-old son Tim and patted the boy on the head.

"Don't worry," he said, as father and son made their way out of the arena. "We'll be back."

9

32-0—NCAA Champs

The sign that hung in the Indiana dressing room was a reminder of how the '74–75 season had been rendered a disappointment.

KENTUCKY 92 INDIANA 90
OUR DEFENSE WAS RESPONSIBLE
FOR THIS

It was a new season, and Bobby Knight was on the case. Coach was determined that the 1975–76 season would fulfill the promise of this Hoosier team—that his boys would not come up short as they had against Kentucky the year before. Only an NCAA title would vindicate this group.

Green and the Super Sub Laskowski were

graduated from the '74–75 squad. Abernethy would move into Green's slot and reserves Jim Crews, Jim Wisman, Wayne Radford and Rich Valavicius would provide bench strength.

It was no secret that with Abernethy, May, Buckner, Benson and Wilkerson returning the Hoosiers were loaded. "Indiana has the best team with the best players and the best coach," Marquette coach Al McGuire told newsmen before the season even began. In its college basketball preview issue, *Sports Illustrated* confirmed that widespread impression, ranking Indiana #1, the best team in the country. Tongue-in-cheek, SI noted:

> Indiana practices are more closely guarded than a Howard Hughes hideaway. Players work out behind a shroud of black curtains, and few visitors are permitted to pass through them, not even $1,000 contributors to the Hoosier Hundred Club. The reason stems from the charity in Coach Bob Knight's heart: a stray opponent stumbling onto the scene might lapse into terminal depression at the sight of how good Indiana looks.

But reputation was no guarantee. Many a vaunted team had cracked under the pressure of living up to its promise. Whether Indiana would succumb remained to be seen. As the team-to-beat, the Hoosiers were a target. Opponents would prime themselves for I-U, eager to knock the kingpin off his mantle.

Knight knew his was a special team. But he also knew the vagaries of a long season could undermine any squad. The late-season injury to May was a profound reminder of the delicate balance on which success rode. While I-U partisans might put the team's loss to Kentucky to May's diminished capacity, that was no solace to Knight.

But Knight would take comfort from the team's opening game in '75–76, against defending NCAA champion UCLA, the last of the ten Bruin champions coached by John Wooden. Wooden had retired after the '74–75 season, bequeathing the team to new coach Gene Bartow. In its preseason poll, *Sports Illustrated* had ranked UCLA #2, and spoken glowingly of its core group of Richard Washington, Andre Mc-Carter and Marques Johnson.

But Indiana astonished a sellout crowd of 19,115 in St. Louis Arena and a nationwide television audience as it took apart UCLA with surgical precision. It was 36–28 at halftime when the Hoosiers got serious. Buckner scored I-U's

first eight points of the second half in less than
two minutes to increase the lead to 44–30. UCLA
had no chance after that. May would hit 15 of his
24 shots and end up with a game-high 33 points.
Benson would score 17 points and pull down 14
rebounds. And Indiana would romp 84–64,
prompting writer Barry McDermott to say:

> Even John Wooden would have had to
> check the dental records to identify what
> was left of UCLA. His old team looked as
> if it had been staring down both barrels of
> a shotgun when Indiana pulled the trigger.
> The blast shattered a dynasty.

Even as his troops pounded UCLA, Knight
could not relax. During the game he would argue
with the official scorer about the number of time-
outs he had, kick over a chair in anger and refrain
from sending in the scrubs until there was less
than a minute remaining in the game.

The Hoosiers left their next opponent, Florida
State, feeling just as abused as UCLA, taking a
47–20 halftime lead and going on to win 83–59.

"I'm glad this isn't like baseball," quipped
Florida State coach Hugh Durham afterward.
"I'd hate to play these guys in a three-game
homestand."

So it went. Once again, Indiana in the regular season was unbeatable. Oh, there was the occasional close game—overtime squeakers against Kentucky and Michigan—but mostly the Hoosiers steamrollered their foes. Pounded Virginia Tech 101–74. Routed Columbia 106–63. Romped against Manhattan 97–61. Laid into Illinois 83–55. Destroyed Wisconsin 114–61. Twenty-seven straight victories in the regular season.

For Knight, it had been a dream season, with a minimum of muss-n-fuss from the coach—only one truly untoward incident that might have come and gone if Knight hadn't made an issue of it.

The incident had occurred during Indiana's February 7, 1976, game against Michigan, shortly before the end of the first half. When reserve guard, Jim Wisman, committed a couples of miscues against the Wolverines' press, Knight called a time-out and then, walking onto the court, grabbed Wisman by his jersey and yanked him toward the bench and into a chair.

The moment of the jersey-clutch was captured by an *Indianapolis Star* photographer, Jerry Clark. The photo was front page the next day in the *Star,* and was picked up by the Associated Press and United Press International and circulated across the country.

By 1976, Knight was a sworn enemy of the

press, regularly issuing contemptuous remarks about their inadequacies and treating them in news conferences with disdain or simply going AWOL after games.

It hadn't always been that way, as veteran reporter Dennis Royalty remembered. Royalty, who had covered the team for the *Bloomington Courier-Tribune* (which went defunct in 1973) in Knight's early years at I-U, recalled a newcomer coach who, as he put it, "spoke TO people, not down to them." That Bobby Knight—while prone to the occasional outburst—had a more reasonable attitude about the men who covered the I-U basketball beat. He permitted Royalty to watch the team practice and was always available to reporters after the game.

But, as Royalty would observe in a column for the *Indianapolis Star* years later, Knight withdrew from and held himself above contact with the media.

> One of my last contacts with the coach was a letter I sent that was critical of the way he'd cut off the press after games. I urged him to reverse the decision. The response was a polite "no thanks. . . ." I sent the letter because I was concerned that he was isolating himself from popular opin-

ion and lifting himself beyond questioning.

Ever notice how the truly great people
in life treat everyone? By that standard,
Knight no longer measured up.

When Bobby Knight saw that front-page picture in the Star of him grabbing Wisman by his
jersey, he was not happy. He viewed it as negative coverage and said so on his weekly TV show
the day after the incident. Why one flawed moment in a game filled with many great moments?
he wondered. Why couldn't the paper have published a picture of Kent Benson tipping in the
basket that sent the game into overtime? he
asked.

He also apologized for grabbing Wisman:
"The thing I realized quicker than anybody there
was that I had made a mistake. You know I've
never grabbed a ballplayer in 11 years of coaching. My standard procedure when a kid comes
out of a game—no matter how poorly he's
played—is to whack that kid on the rear end. I've
never seen this picture anywhere. So one time in
11 years I grab a kid by the shirt and I sit him
down. As soon as the game is over, I went up to
him and said, 'Jimmy, there's no way I should
have grabbed your shirt. I'm really sorry about

doing it. You know I didn't do it to embarrass you. I was just very upset. You were hurting the team at the time.' That was my reaction. I said I was sorry."

Knight's comments triggered a flood of angry phone calls to the Star office and prompted support of Knight in the rival *Indianapolis News*. The *News'* assistant managing editor, Wendell Trogdon, weighed in with a front-page "commentary" in which he defended Knight and argued that college basketball is a business, not a sport. Trogdon asserted that Knight had done his job by making basketball a paying proposition.

> So Knight is a little rough on his players. So what? They've all had the mettle to take it and come back for more. That's what life is all about, and that's why coach Knight's players will be successful long after they hang up their jerseys with his fingerprints on them.

In his own paper, Trogdon's column drew a quick rebuttal from the *News*'s sports editor, Wayne Fuson, who pointed out that John Wooden and Branch McCracken were great coaches too, and neither resorted to jerking a player around by his jersey. Added Fuson:

It's a pity that Knight can't control his emotions better. Even Knight knew it was wrong and apologized. And if college basketball has gotten to the point, as Trogdon contends, that it's a business in which such actions are okay, then educators had better take a look at the situation. Winning at any price has no place in college sports.

Meanwhile, over at the *Star* the paper's sports editor, Bob Collins, was discovering that he had a controversy brewing.

"Up until 6:30 that evening when Knight's show came on, we hadn't received a single call about the picture," Collins would recall. "At a quarter of seven, my phone, which is listed, started ringing at home and the phones at the paper kept ringing for 48 hours."

Since the calls to Collins were nearly unanimous in their support of Knight, the *Star*'s sports editor decided the callers might better convey their sentiments directly to Knight. He published Knight's unlisted home phone number. Knight's supporters did indeed call, in numbers that required the coach to change his number.

Said Collins: "I knew full well that Bobby would have his number changed the very next morning. He hasn't caught any heat at all, but I'm still catching it. Will Bobby Knight give his home phone number to people? Everybody knows mine. It's in the phone book.

"Look, Knight could charm the tits off a snake if he wanted to. But he has what I call a childish, uncontrollable temper. He has this Nixon complex that the press is out to get him."

Knight denied that, saying: "I have great respect for people who can write to begin with. With that thought in mind, I've always gotten along pretty well with people in the press. But then I've not hesitated to tell people in the press when I think they're wrong or that I think they don't know what they're talking about."

At the first practice after the jersey-pull brouhaha, Knight tried to make light of the temper display with Wisman. "I told Jimmy," he said, "either he had better learn our press offense or get a tear-away shirt."

On February 24, 1976, during ceremonies honoring I-U's seniors before they went out to play Illinois, Knight drew laughs when the microphone went on the blink and he quipped: "This must have been set up by the *Indianapolis Star*."

27–0 for the second straight year Indiana had gone through its regular-season schedule undefeated.

But without an NCAA championship, Knight and his players knew, the unbeaten mark would be a hollow accomplishment. The pressure was on the Hoosiers to win it all.

First-round opponent, St. John's, provided no serious obstacle: Indiana won 90–70.

Southeastern Conference champion Alabama would prove far more formidable a foe in I-U's next game. With 3:58 to play in the game, a 'Bama basket gave it the lead, 69–68. Indiana went back ahead at 2:02 when May hit a 17-foot jump shot that made the score 70–69. Then the Hoosier defense dug in, not allowing the Crimson Tide to get off another shot down the stretch. Shutting down the Alabama offense, Indiana went on to win 74–69.

Marquette was next. Coach Al McGuire's team got close—to within three points with 25 seconds remaining. But that was when McGuire was assessed his second technical foul of the game. Indiana took advantage of McGuire's outburst, winning the Mideast regional, 65–56.

The final four would be comprised of Indiana, UCLA, Michigan and an undefeated Rutgers team.

UCLA, spoiling for revenge after its opening-game demolition by the Hoosiers, was an improved squad when the two teams met in the

NCAAs. After losing its opening game to Indiana, the Bruins had regrouped, winning the Pac-Eight and then moving easily through the West Regional.

The game got off on an ominous note for I-U. Barely two minutes into the contest, UCLA shot ahead 7–2 as Richard Washington scored 5 points and drew two quick personal fouls on Benson. Knight called time-out and shifted Abernethy on to Washington. Abernethy shut down Washington, who did not score again until there were 13 minutes left in the game.

By then Indiana had figured out that UCLA lacked an outside shooting threat and that by clogging the middle it could contain Marques Johnson and force Washington to wander out to the perimeter for the basketball. The Hoosiers won 65–51.

Meanwhile, Michigan had knocked off previously unbeaten (31–0) Rutgers, 86–70, which meant the championship game would be an all-Big Ten affair. That game would take place in Philadelphia's Spectrum on March 29, 1976, on the same night the Oscars ceremony was being held in Los Angeles.

The game would not start well for Indiana. A year after its hopes had been dealt a cruel blow when May shattered his forearm, the Hoosiers would see their chances jeopardized again by injury, this time to Bobby Wilkerson and with the game not three minutes old.

At 17:17 of the first half, Michigan's Wayman Britt drove hard to the basket and caught defensive specialist Wilkerson with an elbow that knocked Wilkerson unconscious while giving the Wolverines a 6–4 lead . For almost 15 minutes, medical personnel attended to Wilkerson on the Spectrum floor.

Officials ruled the collision an accident and called no foul. Wilkerson was gone, and would not play any more on this night. The specter of another snakebitten season loomed for the Hoosiers.

But before a Spectrum crowd of 17,540, Indiana did not fold. Knight replaced Wilkerson with Wisman, the same player whose jersey he had grabbed in a regular-season game against these Wolverines. But Wisman came through in the big game. As Michigan guard Steve Grote said, "Indiana couldn't hit the first pass to the wing to get into its offense. Then Wisman came in and they started to run their game and to muscle us."

Still, at halftime Michigan led 34–29, thanks to torrid 61.5 percent shooting. But Indiana rallied. Five minutes into the second half, the score was tied. And after the Hoosiers fouled out Michigan's big man, Phil Hubbard with 7:27 left, they were home free.

In Hollywood, as Eliot Gould and Isabelle Adjani were in the process of presenting one of the coveted Oscars for the year's best film, Ms. Adjani said, "and the winner is."

To which Gould immediately quipped: "Indiana, 86–68."

In Hollywood, Steven Spielberg's *Jaws* was a winner. In Philadelphia, it was Bobby Knight's Hoosiers. 32–0—and an NCAA title. Yes, Bobby Knight had reached the pinnacle of his profession. Indiana was the best college team in the land.

In the second half, the Hoosiers had hit 60 percent of their shots while holding Michigan to 36 percent from the floor. May nailed 10 of 17 from the floor and 6 of 6 from the free throw line for 26 points. Benson made 11 of 20 shots from the floor and 3 of 5 from the foul line for 25 points. The deed was done.

Out on the Spectrum floor, Buckner came flying through the air, leaping into Knight's arms.

May hugged his coach and told him: "We finally beat 'em, baby."

Afterward, Knight would tell newsmen: "It's been a two-year quest for us. These kids are very, very deserving. I know better than anybody how hard and how long they have worked for this. I've never been so proud as I have been of these kids."

They were not just words to Knight. Through the years that followed, through good times and bad, this '75–76 team would hold a special place in his heart. The squad had played Bobby Knight's kind of basketball, and played it better than any group he would coach.

But for Knight, while victory was sweet, it was just a moment in time. There would be seasons and seasons to go.

10

The Battle of San Juan

Pat Knight had not been a sports fan, hadn't related to his son's passion for basketball. When Bobby suited up for Orrville High games, his father was a no-show at the Red Riders' games.

But what Pat Knight conferred on Bobby was a love of the outdoors—of hunting and fishing.

In the years that followed, the coach's antidote to the tumults of a basketball season was to lose himself in nature. He would leave the family's one-story house on three woodsy acres just outside of Bloomington and off he'd go—west to Montana, Idaho, New Mexico—anywhere where a man could feel himself subsumed by the great outdoors.

Sometimes he went alone. Other times he might invite his old Orrville basketball coach,

Jack Graham, who lived in Boulder, Colorado, to meet him in Durango to fish. Or ask Orrville friends like Dave Knight (no relation) or Dr. Dick Rhodes to be his hunting partners. In later years, his sons Tim and Pat went along on these outdoors excursions. Once Knight and his boyhood hero, Red Sox slugger Ted Williams—himself a reknowned angler, fished together in Russia.

For Knight fishing let him retreat from the go-go life of a basketball coach, if only briefly.

"It's quiet and people can't get to you," he said, "and there's competitiveness to fishing. If you get everything together and catch the fish, it's like putting everything together to win a basketball game."

Knight claimed that once he caught the fish, he threw it back. The challenge of landing it was what compelled him.

As for hunting birds, Knight justified the killing by saying, "The life span of a bird is 13 months. I never hunt deer or anything else; I hunt quail, and quail have to be thinned out for new broods. There are people who abuse hunting, but it is a very essential part of the natural balance."

At I-U, the thinning of the ranks—Buckner, Wilkerson, May and Abernethy all graduated— brought a kind of natural balance to college ball. Indiana, which had dominated the sport by winning 61 of 62 games over two seasons, was suddenly just another team. Knight recoiled when writers referred to the '76–77 team as NCAA defending champions, saying, "We're really not the defending champions. This team didn't win the national championship. Give me Buckner, May, Wilkerson and that team and we'll defend the national championship."

With Benson the only starter returning from that championship team, I-U proved vulnerable, losing early and often, even to lowly Toledo. It did not help that Benson—the heart of this team—would miss I-U's last four games after suffering an injury that would require back surgery. The '76–77 squad went 16–11.

For Knight, it was his worst season since 1970–71, his last year at Army, when the Cadets had gone 11–13, in what would be the coach's only losing season. The Hoosiers did better in '77–78, with a record of 21–8 and a post-season NCAA berth. I-U beat Furman 63–62 in its opening-round game but lost a 61–60 heartbreaker to Villanova in its next contest, ending the season.

Early into the next season, 1978–79, the team's ranks were thinned under controversial circumstances. In an era when the youth culture adopted long hair, mustaches and beards and were given to casual drug use, Knight stood for the old verities. For Coach, neatness counted. He didn't allow the counter-culture look on his squad. No long hair. No mustaches. When the team traveled, players dressed in blazers.

In November, at the start of the '78–79 season, Knight learned that players of his allegedly had smoked marijuana before and after games in the Sea Wolf Classic in Anchorage, Alaska, where the Hoosiers had lost to Pepperdine and Texas A&M. Some reports said that Knight had walked in on a party and discovered the boys smoking the wacky weed; other reports said that he had heard about it second-hand, through a player of his.

Whatever. Knight confronted the suspect players and as a result three of them—Tommy Baker, a six-foot-two sophomore guard averaging 7.2 points per game; Jim Roberson, a six-foot-nine senior forward averaging 3.5 points per game and Dan Cox, a six-foot-six sophomore swing man averaging 2 points per game—were dismissed from the team. Five others—Ray Tolbert, a six-foot-nine sophomore center and the team's leading scorer with a 14.2 points per game average; Landon Turner, a six-foot-nine freshman center averaging 1.7 points per game; Mike Woodson, a six-foot-five junior forward averaging 12.2 points per game; Phil Isenbarger, a six-foot-eight sophomore forward averaging 2.2 points per game; and Eric Kirchner, a six-foot-seven sophomore forward averaging 1.3 points per game—were placed on indefinite probation.

Word of Knight's decision appeared first in the campus paper, the December 12th edition of the *Indiana Daily Student*. A day later, a follow-up story appeared in the *IDS* under a headline that read: "POT USE POSSIBLY LED TO DISMISSALS. Student stringers from the IDS alerted newspapers in Louisville and Evansville.

At first I-U and Knight adopted a policy of silence, refusing to comment. But as the media kept poking at the story, they were obliged to go public. Knight would not specify the reason for what he had done, very likely because of privacy regulations that prohibited the school from detailing dismissal information without the student's permission. But when he did discuss the situation, he was no shrinking violet about his forthright stance.

"I'll tell you what I think, and this sounds egotistical, but I'm the only guy coaching today who will stand up and do something," Knight said. "If I had to, I'd kick three off the next year, and three the next year and three the next, if it was a matter of principle."

For a while, none of the parties involved

would say outright that the dismissed players had smoked marijuana. For instance, when a reporter asked Baker had marijuana been the reason for dismissal, he replied, "You can say that in your story, but I won't say it for you. It has something to do with Alaska, but it goes farther than that. What happened there was just part of it. It was building fora long time. You would have to dig real deep into the team to really know what is going on."

On December 13, Tom Campbell of WISH-TV in Indianapolis interviewed Roberson in Bloomington. During the course of a lengthy interview, Campbell asked, "What really happened. Can you pinpoint it? Was it marijuana?"

Replied Roberson: "Yeah, it was. That was it, straight."

Knight's actions were roundly praised by the establishment. Fuson, the *Indiana News*'s sports editor, wrote:

> The Indiana situation should serve as a numbing example for other athletes throughout the nation. Every attempt must be made to keep sport clean, even though athletes are tempted at every turn. Just because others violate rules and get by with it is no excuse.

The other side of the issue was represented by the reaction of an I-U student who, when interviewed, said: "It's time Bobby Knight joined the 20th century."

The dismissal of Roberson, Cox and Baker brought to ten the number of players who had left the I-U team—voluntarily or involuntarily— since the Hoosiers won the NCAA title in 1976.

First it was six-foot-eight Mark Haymore, who transferred to Massachusetts because he said he didn't like the atmosphere at Indiana.

Next, Bob Bender, a six-foot-three guard, went to Duke because he felt he'd get more playing time there.

Six-foot-five swingman Trent Smock who rejoined the basketball team after playing on the football team, was dismissed, he said, because he questioned his role on the team.

Mike Miday, a six-foot-eight forward, who transferred to Bowling Green, left Indiana because he "could not stand the way he [Knight] treated me as a human being." Miday said his knees would shake when Knight upbraided him. "I usually have confidence in my playing, but every game I went out there I was playing in fear of him."

Six-foot-five Rich Valavicius, a transfer to Auburn, hinted his decision to leave had to do with Knight's coaching techniques.

Derek Holcomb, a six-foot-eleven center who transferred to Illinois, said Knight's program "just didn't suit my lifestyle like I thought it would."

Six-foot-four Billy Cunningham had played eight games the previous season, then moved on to UNLV.

While none of the defectors had been stars, some of them had been contributors to the team's success. That Knight's disciplined, often abusive style had chased more than a few of them away was obvious. It was not then, nor would be in the years that followed, easy to co-exist with this coach. Knight got in players' faces, instilling an atmosphere of fear. He rode some of them mercilessly. His objective, he said, was to push them beyond their perceived limits: "I'll tell my players, 'You're not playing a team, you're playing the game of basketball. Your opponent is yourself, your potential.' "

It was a question of values. Players who left I-U because of Knight viewed their coach's excesses as not worth the bother. For them, the game ceased to be fun when their self-image was assailed on a nearly daily basis.

Those who stayed the course, who played their four years for Knight, were like marine boot-camp survivors. They had withstood the rigors and rages of their coach and, they like to believed, were better men and better players for it, even if, in looking back, a few might concede they still felt uneasy about certain moments when Knight embarrassed them.

A couple of years after he left I-U, Kent Benson, for instance, still recalled a night in the Sugar Bowl tournament in New Orleans when Knight humiliated him. "He kept telling me to get off my feet," said Benson. "He even benched me. I don't agree with the way he handles players personally, but I think Coach Knight is the best coach who ever lived. He will go through a brick wall for his players. He gave us 100 percent. He stayed up all hours trying to make us a better ball team. If I had to do it all over again, knowing Coach Knight, I still would have gone to Indiana to play for him."

None of them—survivors or defectors—would question Knight's drive, his dedication, his knowledge of the game. None would say he couldn't make a group of strangers play like the quintessential team. He could, in the idiom of the hyperbolic Dick Vitale, "flat out coach." But for every player it came down to this: Was Bobby Knight worth the trouble?

By the late 70s, he had not changed. Never mind that Knight had coached an NCAA champion. He was not the sort to rest on his laurels. No, Knight continued to be Knight—a man who on or off the basketball court was trigger-tempered, outspoken and sometimes confrontational beyond reason.

As a coach, he was able to channel those dark impulses into winning teams. Enough players went along with the program. Only two years after his worst season at I-U, his '78–79 Hoosiers—led by Woodson (21 points per game) and Tolbert (12 points per game)—went 22–12 and won the NIT.

Away from the court, though, Knight's rage sometimes appeared to exacerbate situations that needn't happen—had he the grace and the common sense to lighten up. But Knight had an attack-dog aggression—a compelling need to have the last word. Even those closest to him, who knew Knight as a supportive friend and a charitable man, would shake their heads at how perverse he could be when push came to shove. As John Flynn, a newspaper man who went back with Knight to his days as a coach at Cuyahoga Falls and had remained his friend, would say: "Bob Knight is an asshole, but he knows it and tries like hell to make up for it."

In May '79, soon after the season had ended, Knight became embroiled in a shouting match with a bicyclist in the middle of a Bloomington street. Things grew worse when Knight noticed that a photographer who was there by chance was snapping away. When Knight demanded that the photographer, Bill Warren, a student on the staff of the campus newspaper, stop shooting and Warren refused, Knight allegedly shoved him over a hedgerow.

That tendency of his to make a bad situation worse was underscored when Knight agreed to coach the United States team at the Pan American Games in Puerto Rico in July 1979.

On April 22, the team gathered in Bloomington. There Knight began drilling a squad that included two I-U juniors, Mike Woodson and Ray Tolbert, and collegians like Michael Brooks (La-Salle), Kevin McHale (Minnesota), Ronnie Lester (Iowa), Mike O'Koren (North Carolina), Kyle Macy (Kentucky), Sam Clancy (Iowa), John Duren (Georgetown) and Danny Vranes (Utah). Knight carried two high school players as well, seven-foot-three Ralph Sampson, who was bound for the University of Virginia that fall, and Isiah Thomas, a talented guard out of Chicago, whom Knight had recruited for Indiana.

In the months preceding the team's arrival in

San Juan, Knight would work the players hard, his fire-breathing intensity leading O'Koren to say: "It's not a question of whether we like Coach Knight or not. We heard all the stories about him and came out for the team anyway, because we wanted to represent the U.S. We knew he was demanding and strict, but he wins. We've talked among ourselves quite a bit, and we decided that he's just different from everyone else's coach."

Knight's troubles in Puerto Rico started on July 2, with the team's opening-game 113–88 rout of the Virgin Islands. Knight was called for a technical foul and then ejected from the arena when he came onto the court to argue his case with the Spanish-speaking officials, Calvin Pacheco of Puerto Rico and Pedro Escobedo of Mexico.

The next morning, he was called before representatives of the International Amateur Basketball Federation and warned that further misbehavior would be grounds for expulsion of the U.S. team.

"They gave him a scolding," said Robert Kane, the president of the United States Olympic Committee, who attended the meeting.

That night, before a capacity crowd of 4,000, the United States beat Cuba 85–53. But Knight's pleasure in the victory was diminished when Cuba's Tomas Herrera punched Macy and fractured his jaw during the blowout. Knight found it odd that the incident drew little press coverage— odd considering that Herrera twice before had gotten into fights with American players during international competitions.

But to him that seemed to fit the anti-American atmosphere of the games, where on opening day at least one American flag was burnt— Knight contradicted those reports when he said not one but five American flags went up in flames.

Meanwhile, Knight himself continued to flame, haranguing his players during games, his outbursts extreme enough that courtsiders unfamiliar with the coach were taken aback. When he blew up at Isiah Thomas, after the 18-year-old future Hoosier missed a dunk with the United States leading Brazil by 14 points, the level of his rage incensed some spectators, who shouted for Thomas to hit the coach.

But it wasn't until July 8th that push came to shove for Knight. At 10:45 that morning, as an hour-long practice session for the American team was drawing to a close at the Espiritu Santo High School, outside San Juan, the Brazilian women's team arrived at the gym. The Brazilians, early for

their 11 o'clock practice, were noisy enough
while they waited to disconcert Knight. He had
his assistant coach, Mike Kryzewski, ask Jose de
Silva, the 33-year-old patrolman guarding the
gym entrance, why the Brazilian team was let in
early.

What happened from that moment on would
be shrouded in conflicting versions.

Knight would claim—and Krzyzewski would
corroborate—that de Silva's reply was: "Hey,
man, when you're in Puerto Rico you do as I
say."

Knight said he then told the Brazilians, "Hey.
We have the gym until 11. If you're not gonna be
quiet you've got to get the hell out of here."

At that point, de Silva told the Americans, "I
say that they stay."

Did Knight call the Brazilians "whores" and
call de Silva a "nigger" as the patrolman later
claimed?

Knight denied uttering either of those words
and claimed that as he and de Silva argued, the
policeman began wagging his finger in the
coach's face, and ended up poking him in the eye.
That triggered a reflex response, said Knight, re-
sulting in the coach's pushing him away with the
heel of his hand against de Silva's chin.

De Silva would deny poking Knight in the eye
and would accuse him of first violence.

Neither side would dispute what happened next.

An angry De Silva told Knight: "This isn't the United States. This is Puerto Rico. You hit a policeman. You're under arrest."

In the parking lot outside the school, the coach claimed, de Silva took a night stick from his unmarked car, pushed it against Knight's nose and said, "Goddamn you, brother, this is what I'd like to use on you. You want me to use this on you, don't you?"

Knight was handcuffed, jailed and within the hour freed, with police telling U.S. officials no charges would be pressed.

But de Silva was not about to let Knight go scott-free. The next day, he filed assault charges in San Juan District Court. Knight counterfiled, charging de Silva with assault and battery, violation of civil rights and incarceration without knowledge of the charges.

San Juan district judge Rafael Rieskohl not only dismissed Knight's countercharges, but he ordered the coach to stand trial later that week, on Friday the 13th. Knight's attorneys sought and got the court date changed to August 22, leaving the coach free to tend to his team. If convicted Knight was looking at fines ranging from $50 to $500 and a jail sentence ranging from one day to six months. Or both.

Back in the States, friends of Knight sought out Indiana politicians to see if they could help get the case quashed. But by now Puerto Rican national pride was involved, and no amount of coaxing from influential Americans would sway de Silva.

That Friday the 13th, the undefeated United States team met host Puerto Rico in the gold-medal final at Roberto Clemente Coliseum. The arena, which usually held 9,600 fans, was far over capacity with an estimated 12,000 spectators being shoehorned in.

Knight was greeted by boos, but was deadpan before the jeering crowd. The U.S. took a 15-point halftime lead, but Puerto Rico rallied to trail by only 3 points, 71–68, midway through the second half. With the home team's fans waving miniature Puerto Rican flags, beating bongos, stomping their feet and clapping, young Isiah Thomas quickly squelched their expectations. Over the next four minutes, he took command of the game, scoring three baskets, handing out two assists and blocking a shot—an offensive surge that gave the U.S. a 10-point lead. Puerto Rico was finished. The U.S. went on to win 113–94 as the Indiana-bound high school kid scored 20 points and earned praise from Knight, who in the final moments put his arm around Thomas and told him, "I'm proud of you."

When the game ended and his players hoisted a tearful Knight onto their shoulders, Knight responded now to the boos of the crowd by repeatedly thrusting his right index finger into the air—the time-honored we're-number-one gesture.

He wasn't finished, though. Not by a long shot. As the players lined up to receive their gold medals, Knight watched from a corner of the floor, reacting to the continuing jeers and boos by telling several American reporters: "Fuck 'em. Fuck 'em all. I'll tell you what. Their basketball team is a helluva lot easier to beat than their court system. The only fucking thing they know how to do is grow bananas."

At the news conference afterward, mistaking Jenny Kellner, a United Press International reporter, for Puerto Rican, Knight delivered an anti-Puerto Rican diatribe.

Said Kellner: "I would be proud to be Puerto Rican and I have Puerto Rican friends. But when I realized he acted like that because he thought I was Puerto Rican I started to cry. When Knight found out I wasn't Puerto Rican, he came over and apologized, but I still feel terrible about the incident."

There was more. When Knight remarked, "I didn't have any friends in Puerto Rico when I came here, so I don't have any fewer when I leave," it set off Genaro Marchand, Puerto Rico's delegate to the International Amateur Basketball Federation.

"You treat us like dirt," Marchand told him. "You have said nothing but bad things since you got here. You are an embarrassment to America, our country." As Knight made his exit, Marchand's parting shot was: "You are an ugly American."

Back in the States, Knight told the press he didn't think there was a chance of getting justice in San Juan.

"I don't think I could win down there if I had Clarence Darrow for a defense attorney and Jesus Christ as a character witness," he said.

Knight said his Puerto Rican attorneys had wanted him to plead guilty.

"I told them to stick it," he said. "There was no way I was going to plead guilty for something I didn't do just to get it over with. It would be a mockery. It's absolutely ridiculous."

Knight's sentiments dictated how his American defense attorneys would proceed: a trial in absence of the defendant—a recourse allowed by Puerto Rican law.

In Indiana, as the days preceding the trial unfolded, Knight had plenty of supporters. One of them, Ann White, who owned "Annie B's Screened Fabrics store," created T-shirts that said, "FREE BOBBY KNIGHT" on the front and on the back "REMEMBER SAN JUAN." She did a brisk business in these red-and-white shirts, numbering among her customers Nancy Knight, the coach's wife.

"At first we were concerned that people might think we were taking advantage of a bad situation," White told a reporter. "But Nancy's reaction was favorable and everybody is so much behind Bobby. The shirts were taken in that vein."

On August 22, district court judge Rurico Rivera heard the case in San Juan. De Silva testified that Knight had reacted to the arrival of the Brazilian women by shouting: "Get these dirty whores out of here."

De Silva said he told Knight: "You can't talk about ladies like that."

The police officer stated Knight's response was: "To hell with them. And to hell with you, too. Get your ass out of here."

De Silva testified that there was a fracas between Knight and him, and when the officer placed his hand on Knight's arm, the coach yelled: "Get your dirty hands off me, nigger."

De Silva said that the coach punched him on

the left side of the face while he was writing Knight's name on a pad and preparing to arrest him.

Knight was found guilty, in absentia, of assaulting de Silva and was given the maximum sentence—six months in jail and a $500 fine.

Knight, who was vacationing in Montana at the time, gave this statement to Bob Hammel of the *Bloomington Herald-Telephone:*

> Even forgetting the truth or validity of the charges, it would be interesting to know the last time anyone got the maximum penalty for a misdemeanor.
>
> In my thinking, there was no way there was any chance to win, even if we took everybody down there. We filed charges, and the D.A. wouldn't listen. The cop was lying, so what the hell chance did I have? I told Clarence Doninger and Steve Ferguson [Knight's American attorneys] it would be a waste of time and money. . . .
>
> I offered my resignation at Indiana University because the university has to have the opportunity to do what it freely and clearly thinks is best for Indiana University. It isn't my desire to do anything other than coach basketball at Indiana University. That isn't mine to say.

There is no question in my mind that if I had gone to Puerto Rico I would be in jail. The sentence would be exactly the same. There is a feeling of helplessness in view of what transpired.

Indiana University president John Ryan said he would not accept Knight's offer to resign. But Chris Gambil, the student body president, said that while he agreed with Ryan's decision, he was more concerned with derogatory quotes attributed to Knight after the gold-medal victory over Puerto Rico. Gambil said he would like to see measures taken to avoid a repetition of such incidents.

"If the university does not draw a line and say, 'You have to operate within this box,' a serious incident will come up again," Gambil said. "If that's the case, then the university's got to consider letting him go. Now would be just a real opportune time to draw the box and say, 'Here's what you have to do to continue as coach'. Is Knight a guy who can live with the rules? I think there's some reason to doubt that."

11

The Little Team
That Could

As the 1979–80 college basketball season loomed, Robert Montgomery Knight had put together another Hoosier powerhouse—a team that had the potential to challenge for a national title. Like that paradigm of Knight-coached teams, his 1975–76 NCAA championship club, this group was loaded ~~with players~~ who would move from the college ranks into the NBA.

Mike Woodson, a six-foot-five senior, would play 13 seasons with New York, New Jersey, Kansas City, Sacramento, the Los Angeles Clippers, Houston and Cleveland and average 14 points per game.

Butch Carter, a six-foot-five senior, would play six seasons with Los Angeles, Indiana, New

York and Philadelphia and average 8.7 points per game.

Ray Tolbert, a six-foot-nine junior, would play five seasons with New Jersey, Seattle, Detroit, New York, the Los Angeles Lakers and Atlanta and would average 3.6 points per game.

Randy Wittman, a six-foot-six sophomore, would play nine seasons with Atlanta, Sacramento and Indiana and average 7.4 points per game.

Jim Thomas, a six-foot-three freshman, would play three seasons with Indiana and the Los Angeles Clippers and average 8.6 points per game.

Isiah Thomas, a six-foot-one freshman, would play 13 seasons with Detroit and average 19.2 points per game while leading the Pistons to two NBA championships, in 1990 and 1991.

In its college basketball preview issue, *Sports Illustrated* rated Indiana its number one team:

> This is not an overpowering Indiana team like the one that blitzed through an unbeaten season to the national title in 1976. But it is considerably better than the one that won the NIT last March.

Isiah Lord Thomas III, fresh out of St. Joseph's High School in Westchester, Illinois, was key to the Hoosiers' chances. He was unlike any player Knight had had—more naturally talented and with a knack for making plays on his own. Thomas was a freewheeler whose very style was the antithesis of Knight's conservative ball-control game. Yet Thomas was, Knight knew, a bright youth with loads of character—a player who, he thought, could make necessary adjustments. Knight called him "the best player I've ever recruited."

That recruitment had been a stormy one. When Knight had turned up at the Thomas household in Chicago, one of Isiah's brothers had insulted Knight and nearly provoked a fight with the coach. Thomas was under severe pressure to stay at home and attend DePaul, where a close friend and future NBA player, Mark Aguirre, was matriculating. The lobbying against Indiana was so extreme that Thomas received mail that insisted that Knight tied up his players and beat them.

"It was so crazy," Thomas said, "that no intelligent person could believe them."

Just the same, Thomas's relationship with Knight was often shaky. The coach recognized that Thomas was a special talent and in time Knight would loosen up his offense to give Isiah more opportunity to exploit his quickness and cunning—to take his man one-on-one.

But that license to freelance came with a cost, Knight's inherent conservatism provoking him to lash out at Thomas whenever the frosh star faltered. Indeed, the sniping had started at the Pan Am games when, during a contest against Brazil, Knight had threatened to put Thomas on a plane home. "You ought to go to DePaul, Isiah," Knight yelled, "because you sure as hell aren't going to be an Indiana player playing like that."

Knight's hopes of once again winning an NCAA title in '79–80 would be undermined, as they had been in '74–75, by injuries. Where Scott May had been the victim then, this time two of his Hoosiers were damaged. By mid-December, after only five games, starting guard Randy Wittman suffered a stress fracture to his foot and was sidelined for the season. Then, on December 18, the team's leading scorer, Woodson, notched 19 points against Toledo but was in so much pain that he would miss seven weeks of the campaign while he recovered from surgery to remove a ruptured disc.

Under the circumstances, Knight and the Hoosiers did well. The team went 21–8, won the Big Ten title and went to the NCAA tournament. But after beating Virginia Tech 68–59 in its opening-round game, Indiana was knocked out of the NCAAs by Purdue, 76–69.

The experts who had figured on Indiana winning it all in '79–80 were less optimistic about an Indiana team that had lost Woodson and Carter to graduation for 1980–81.

Given the absence of those two, it didn't take a rocket scientist to recognize that Thomas, who had averaged 14.6 points per game as a freshman, would have to assume a larger role as a sophomore if the Hoosiers were to amount to anything. But Knight wanted to be sure that Thomas did not play out of control. He sent the message loud and clear in practice sessions—haranguing him and even throwing him out of one preseason team workout.

But while Isiah would have freer reign, and would eventually respond well to it, the anticipated help from his big men, particularly six-foot-ten, 240-pound junior Landon Turner, did not materialize and Indiana suffered for it, losing three of its first eight games.

Turner perplexed Knight. Landon was one of the more naturally talented big men Knight had recruited. At Arsenal Technical High School in Indianapolis, he had averaged 21.4 points per game and 15.8 rebounds, and was considered the best center in the state. In fact, there was talk that he might be good enough to go straight to the NBA.

But at Indiana, Turner had been a bust. While he showed flashes of talent—the kid could run and jump—his performance was so inconsistent that it made Knight apoplectic, a state he was always verging on anyway.

Knight tried mightily to induce his big man to live up to his potential. He blistered him in that withering language he used when a player failed him. Cursed him. Coaxed him. Called him a pussy and even stuck a Tampon® in Turner's locker to reinforce his point.

As a freshman, in the finals of the NIT tournament against Purdue, Turner had shown how good he could be. Playing against Joe Barry Carroll, a future NBA center, Turner scored 13 points and had 5 rebounds while putting Carroll into deep freeze on defense.

But here he was two years later and no matter what Knight said or did, come game time the big man just wasn't getting it done. By February, with the Hoosiers scheduled to play Northwestern, Knight was at wit's end with Turner. Nothing he tried brought out the player within. So he called Turner to his office for a heart-to-heart talk.

"I told him," Knight said, "he should go to the NBA because he had a better chance of playing in that league than he ever had playing for us.

A subdued Bobby Knight sits in front of the University of
Indiana NCAA Championship banners after an interview
about the fine and "zero-tolerance" probation he received
in May 15, 2000. *(AP/Wide World Photos/Michael Conroy)*

Bobby Knight, No. 24, for the Ohio State Buckeyes: 1960–61

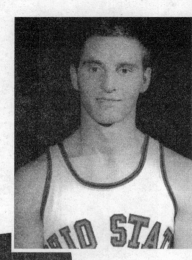

(Photos courtesy of Ohio State University Archives)

Bobby Knight was a One-Man Hurricane

Screaming at an official call.
(Sports Illustrated)

Throwing in the towel—literally—as his team is beaten by
Kentucky 92–90 in the NCAA Mideast Regional Finals in 1975.
(AP/Wide World Photos)

Knight enraged Soviet National Coach, Alexandir Gomelsky (standing left) by banging his shoe on the scorekeeper's table in protest in 1977. *(AP/Wide World Photos)*

The infamous chair-throwing incident during Indiana's 72–63 loss to Purdue in 1975. *(AP/Wide World Photos)*

Never a stranger to controversy, Knight answers questions about his altercation with a Louisiana State fan at a hotel after the semi-finals in 1981. *(AP/Wide World Photos/Gene Puskar)*

Knight's unique style can be amusing . . .

(©Reuters NewMedia Inc./CORBIS)

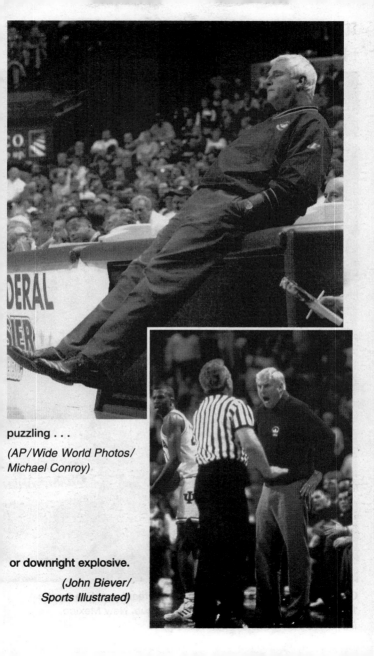

puzzling . . .

(AP/Wide World Photos/ Michael Conroy)

or downright explosive.

(John Biever/ Sports Illustrated)

It was Knight's Way or the Highway

Coach Knight carried a bullwhip during team practice for the 1992 NCAA West Regional in Albuquerque, New Mexico. *(AP/Wide World Photos/Eric Risberg)*

Knight cut his players no slack. He didn't give instructions;
he barked orders at the top of his voice.

Always unpredictable, Knight could play the role of a good-natured uncle, giving advice or just clowning around.

(AP/Wide World Photos/Daniel Hulshizer)

(Rich Clarkson/Sports Illustrated)

(AP/Wide World Photos/ Tom Strattman)

The Winner

From his early years, Knight loved the accolades from his team and fans. *(Sports Illustrated)*

Knight accepts his first NCAA Championship in 1976 with players Scott May and Quinn Buckner. *(AP/Wide World Photos)*

A celebrity in Indiana, his fame spread worldwide when he lead the U.S. Olympic Basketball team to win the gold in 1984. *(©Wally McNamee/CORBIS)*

Like a hero in Ancient Rome, Knight wears the hoop rope from one of his many victories. *(Andrew Bernstein/Sports Illustrated)*

The Loser

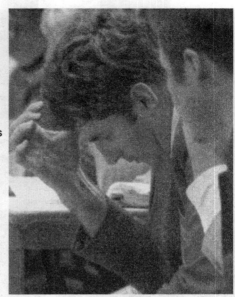

Dejected after his loss in 1975 to Kentucky. *(AP/Wide World Photos)*

Knight pacing the court after his team's humiliating defeat by Purdue in 1998. *(AP/Wide World Photos)*

Coach Bobby Knight, a basketball legend turned pariah. Will he be back? *(AP/Wide World Photos/Tom Strattman)*

He'd gone through this for two and a half years. I said, 'I just don't think you're ever going to play here.' It was the first time I told him, 'Landon, you can't play.' "

It was February 12, 1981, when Indiana played Northwestern, following Knight's blunt conversation with Turner. At the time, the Hoosiers were 14–8 and regarded as a major disappointment. But the Northwestern game would prove a turning point for Landon and the team. Turner entered the game early and committed several miscues that sent him to the bench. But when he was reinserted into the contest later, he hit four of five shots, scored nine points and committed only one foul. For those few minutes, Knight said, "He played as well as I had ever seen him play."

It turned out not to be an isolated instance. Suddenly Turner was the player that Knight had seen in his mind's eye—a force beneath the boards, a lively intelligent player, focused on what had to be done. He was the missing link, the catalytic presence that had pulled a previously struggling team together. Thomas, Tolbert, Turner, Wittman and Ted Kitchell—the I-U starters—began to play at another level. They beat Northwestern that night 86–52 and lost only one more regular-season game in finishing the schedule with a 19–10 record.

But the record did not reflect how good the team really was—or the fact that it had gelled over the stretch run of the regular season. It would remain for the Hoosiers, as Big Ten champions, to show their mettle in the 48-team NCAAs. History was against Indiana, for no team with that many losses had ever won the tournament. But history was an arrangement of facts ever subject to reinvention.

Indiana had no problems in its opening-round game against Maryland, beating the Terps 99–64, as Tolbert scored 26, Turner 20 and Isiah Thomas 19. The Hoosiers made an impression on Maryland coach, Lefty Driesell, who said: "They were the best team since I got my program going. If they had been playing the 76ers, they'd have beaten the 76ers."

By the luck of the draw, the Mideast Regional had been scheduled for Assembly Hall in Bloomington. The Hoosiers did not disappoint the home crowd. On March 20, 1981, they beat Alabama Birmingham 87–72 behind a 27-point night by Isiah Thomas.

Afterward, Alabama Birmingham coach Gene Bartow said, "To me, this was a typical Bob Knight team. They do so many things so well. I didn't see them early this year, but I've heard they were struggling a little then. They're not struggling now."

Nor did they struggle two nights later in the Mideast Regional finals against St. Joseph's, winning easily before a partisan Assembly Hall crowd, 76–46. The Hoosiers were headed for the Final Four in Philadelphia.

Dale Brown's LSU Tigers proved no match for Indiana on Final Four weekend. Although their fans flashed signs indicating that Indiana, like all opponents, was mere "Tiger Bait," the truth was that the tiger was in I-U's tank. Trailing at the half , 30–27, the Hoosiers opened the second half with a 21–4 tear and went on to win 67–49. Turner topped I-U scoring with 20 points.

Indiana was headed for the NCAA championship game against North Carolina. The team that Bobby Knight had called "immature" and "inconsistent" earlier in the season, when the Hoosiers struggled, had grown up.

Meanwhile, back at the Cherry Hill Inn in New Jersey, where the Indiana team and dozens of LSU loyalists were lodged, Knight became entangled in still another of his myriad "incidents." At about 7 P.M., Knight was walking through the hotel lounge when Lewis (Buddy) Bonnecaze, Jr., an LSU fan clad in the team's purple and gold, spotted the coach. Bonnecaze, who was an accountant in real life, called out "congratulations" to Knight for his victory earlier in the day.

Here's Knight's account of what followed:

"When the guy told me congratulations, I said, 'Well, we really weren't Tiger bait after all, were we?'—just in that tone. That's when he stood up and started yelling."

News accounts said that what Bonnecaze yelled was an obscenity, which he repeated when Knight dared him to. Push came to shove when the fan told Knight, again, he was an asshole. Knight threw Bonnecaze against the wall and into a garbage can. And a day later said he wasn't sorry, prompting *New York Times* columnist Dave Anderson to write: "Bobby Knight's teams are supposed to be so disciplined. And they are. But if his players are disciplined, why isn't their coach?"

So much for the coach's Knightmare side. There was a ball game still to play.

North Carolina had upset Ralph Sampson's Virginia squad to advance to the finals against Indiana. The Tarheels featured a front line of future NBA stars—Sam Perkins, James Worthy and Al Wood—and had Jimmy Black and Mike Pepper at the guards. Their coach was Dean Smith. North Carolina-Indiana figured to be a closely contested game.

On game day, March 30, 1981, a hitch developed. In Washington, D.C., President Ronald

Reagan was shot in the chest by a deranged gunman, John Hinckley. For a while Reagan's medical condition raised questions about whether the championship game should be played, or out of respect for Reagan be rescheduled. When reports on the president's condition indicated that his life was in no real danger, NCAA executives decided the game would go on.

"The kids certainly felt as we all did about the tragedy," Knight would say. "But they knew that they had a ball game to play, and they made the adjustment."

Indiana took a 26–25 halftime lead and then broke the game open early in the second half when Isiah Thomas made two quick steals that he converted to baskets. Indiana went on to win 63–50, with Thomas scoring 23 points, 19 in the second half. He was given the tournament's Outstanding Player Award.

Bobby Knight had done it again. His Little-Team-That-Could had confounded statistical probability. Under Knight, the team with nine losses had found its magic just in time. As the team bus headed south the next morning on Highway 37, the sight of folks lined up at crossroads all along the 40-mile stretch from Indianapolis to Bloomington had to be a cheering one for the 40-year-old Knight.

But now that he had reached the pinnacle of his profession, now that he had twice won the NCAA title, did he want to continue this coach's life? Did he want to subject himself to the rigors of perpetual diligence necessary to be successful? Did he want the all-nighters spent looking at game tapes? The torment that filled his heart at the thought of losing? The scrutiny of know-nothing sports columnists? The endless bullshit that went with the Xs and Os of a game he loved?

There were other opportunities out there.

Bobby Knight had been offered coaching jobs in the NBA.

He had said no more than once, although he had been flattered when Red Auerbach—a man he greatly admired—asked if he'd be interested in the Boston Celtic coaching job.

The NBA was not for him, said Knight.

"A college coach," he said, "runs into big enough egos in some high school stars. I can only imagine what it would be like dealing with a player making $400,000 a year. The money has never tempted me because I like the atmosphere around a college campus."

Then there was network TV.

CBS had approached Knight about leaving Indiana to do commentary on its college-basketball telecasts, the network having just acquired the rights to televise the NCAA tournament.

If he wanted the job, Knight would be paid well—reportedly more than double the $200,000 a year he was said to make from his job as coach and the outside income sources that went with being Bobby Knight—the radio and TV shows, the basketball clinics and summer camp.

Already Knight's best player, Isiah Thomas, had snatched his more lucrative opportunity, bolting I-U after two seasons for a four-year contract reportedly worth $1.6 million with the Detroit Pistons.

Was CBS a Plan B that Knight was seriously considering? When asked by reporters, he declined to say one way or the other. But as the *New York Times*'s Malcolm Moran would report:

> After the Hoosiers won the tournament, Knight began discussions with CBS about a multiyear position that would begin this season. He came to meetings with notes and ideas. "Bobby is intrigued by the influence that the business has," said Kevin O'Malley, the executive in charge of college sports. "I think he sits there on Saturday afternoons and listens to

what people say, and bridles at what they say. I think there was a time when he was ready to make the move. That was my impression. . . . Ultimately, I think the accident was one of the very strong influences in his saying, 'I really must remain where I am.' "

The accident.

It had happened on July 25, 1981. Landon Turner had lost control of his car on State Road 46, eight miles east of Columbus, Indiana. The vehicle hit a culvert and turned over.

Anticipating his senior year at I-U and then being a first-round NBA draft choice, Turner now lay paralyzed from the chest down with a broken vertebra.

Knight was on his summer fishing vacation in Idaho when he got word of Turner's accident. He was shattered by the news. As he told Billy Reed of the *Louisville Courier-Journal* soon after: "Nothing has ever affected me like this. To see that kid there in that bed. . . . I've watched this kid four years now, counting his senior year in high school. All that potential, trying to figure out how to get it to explode for him. He was as close to being a totally effective person as he has ever been."

Knight had often been guilty of acting fool-
ishly, making bad situations worse with a perver-
sity beyond logic. Yet the paradox was that
without fanfare he had performed good works—
he'd shown himself to be capable of thoughtful
gestures, of taking command of situations where
others stood idly by.

Knight knew Turner's medical bills were beyond his family's financial reach. So Knight
anointed himself the man responsible for generating funds to see the Turners through their tragedy.
Through Knight, various charity events—softball
games, cookouts, basketball exhibitions, golf
tournaments—were staged to benefit the Landon
Turner Trust Fund.

When a home-run derby was organized at a
minor-league ballpark in Indianapolis, ex-base-
ball star Knight agreed to pitch to 11 of his former players and to Ted Kluzewski, the retired
Cincinnati Reds slugger who had played baseball
and football at Indiana.

In time, $400,000 was raised on Turner's be-
half. Knight would continue to help the player
come to terms with his paralysis, encouraging
him to be around the team and jokingly haranguing him as he had through three years at I-U.
Turner was in his heart, and in his mind. When
Knight happened to spend time with the Celtics'

Auerbach and their coach, Bill Fitch, at an NBA instructional camp in Chicago, he suggested it would be a nice gesture if the Celtics would name Turner as their 10th-round draft choice. Auerbach and Fitch did just that.

"There was a time when I really didn't care for him too much," said Turner. "I just wanted to get the heck out of Indiana University and go on with my life. But once I was hurting and I saw a side of him that I'd never seen before, I developed a love for him."

Turner would go on to earn a B.S. in Physical Education and become a motivational speaker.

Knight would go on to do what came naturally—to coach the game of basketball.

12

Going for Gold

In 1982, the United States Olympics Organizing Committee (USOOC) made an unorthodox choice for the man who would coach the U.S. basketball team at the 1984 Olympics in Los Angeles. Bobby Knight, who had been knee-deep in controversy at the Pan Am Games in Puerto Rico, would lead the Americans.

Predictably, the news provoked second-guessing among sports columnists, who wondered whether Knight could avoid creating another mess. Olympic officials defended Knight, saying that he had been victimized in San Juan—that the patrolman had lied about what had happened and that Knight then had been railroaded by the Puerto Rican judicial system.

Besides, all that was past, wasn't it?

Well, maybe not. In December 1982, at a dinner in Gary, Indiana, where Knight was a speaker, the coach said that on flying out of Puerto Rico he dropped his pants "and placed my bare ass on the window. That's the last thing I wanted those people to see of me."

What Knight didn't know was that a Puerto Rican journalist was in the audience and he reported the incident for the Hispanic Link News Service. As the story spread through mainstream media, it created waves. Sportswriters said— "See, what did I tell you!" And "those people," it turned out, were offended too. Mooning Puerto Rico was not a Puerto Rican's idea of high regard for his people. Congressman Robert Garcia, a Democrat from New York, would write the *New York Times* to say:

I have sent a letter to the United States Olympic Committee and the Los Angeles Olympic Organizing Committee calling for Mr. Knight's removal. In addition, the Congressional Hispanic Caucus and the National Council of La Raza sent letters protesting his appointment.

The problem with Mr. Knight does not stem from his ability as a coach. As an avid sports fan, I appreciate what he has done with the Indiana basketball program. But his behavior off the court is not only adolescent, it is unacceptable. . . .

The Olympic Games, despite recent problems, stand as a symbol of healthy international competition. They attempt to foster understanding among nations, and in particular, the youth of the world. Unfortunately, Coach Knight's remarks at the 1979 Pan Am Games in Puerto Rico led me to believe that he is not supportive of this ideal.

He further complicated the problem by his comments at the banquet in Gary, Indiana. . . . He has proven that he is not capable of representing the United States in any capacity.

The governor of Puerto Rico, Carlos Romero Barcelo, wrote to the USOOC protesting Knight's being chosen to coach the U.S. squad:

First, he set in 1979 a shameful example both in terms of personal conduct and in terms of civic responsibility. And he compounded those transgressions by becoming—as he remains to this day—a fugitive from justice on a conviction for aggravated assault.

Second, Mr. Knight's arrogance and bigotry upstaged and detracted from the fine performances and sportsmanlike conduct of United States coaches and athletes in all the other events held during the Eighth Pan American Games.

Knight's reaction? Hey, it was a joke. I was just kidding around.

"That was a line I made up as a throwaway line to use in these situations that existed everywhere I went relative to Puerto Rico," he said.

William Simon, the president of USOOC, said that although "one can question Bobby's judgment in some of his comments," Knight would remain as Olympic coach—he had "the full support of the U.S. Olympic Committee."

That support was not merely verbal. The USOOC had funded the 1984 men's and women's basketball program for $1 million, up from its budget of $200,000 for the 1972 games.

Nineteen seventy two was the year that game officials had highjacked the gold-medal basketball final, allowing the Russians a re-play of the final seconds that resulted in a reversal of the original outcome—Russia 51, U.S. 50—and the refusal of American players to accept their silver medals.

One of Knight's mentors, Hank Iba, had coached that losing American team and drawn criticism for reigning in his players with a fuddy-duddy conservative style. Knight—ever faithful to his esteemed older coaches—deflected blame from Iba. But the idea of that politicized loss galled Knight, who was a staunch patriot and was determined that history would not repeat itself. Not on Bobby Knight's watch.

Knight approached the '84 Olympics with his usual white-hot resolve. Never mind that so-called experts said that with the pool of graduating college players and undergraduates available to him, the U.S. was can't-miss for a gold medal—that this team might be comparable in talent to the 1960 American squad that had Oscar Robertson, Jerry West, Jerry Lucas, Terry Dischinger and Walter Bellamy. *Los Angeles Times* columnist Jim Murray wrote that on top of that having Knight coach these youngbloods was like "assembling an aircraft carrier to ply the waters between Staten Island and the Battery." In other words, overkill.

It was not how Coach saw it. Sure, there were plenty of talented players out there. But for Knight the pressing issue was to find the right mix—find those 12 players who could fulfill his vision of how this Olympic team should play. As with his Indiana teams, there would be no gold-bricking on defense and attention would be paid on offense to the high-percentage shot.

"I am the coach," said Knight, "and we do things one way. We do it my way."

Knight named as assistant coaches George Raveling of Iowa and Don Donoher of Dayton, and chose Vanderbilt's C. M. Newton as team manager. Together the coaches reviewed tapes of the better international teams—Russia, Yugoslavia, Canada, Italy, Brazil and Spain—and talked about the kind of players that would function best against the style of ball these teams played. Knight and his coaches also discussed the skills and personality quirks of the 72 American players who would be invited to Bloomington that April 16–22, 1984, for the Olympic Trials.

On hand as observers and consultants were coaches of past Olympic teams—Newell ('60), Iba ('64, '68, and '72) Dean Smith ('76) and Dave Gavitt ('80).

The trials were a grind—three practices a day in the stone-cold Indiana field house, on a hard Tartan surface. Knight watched from a Bear Bryant-like tower between the courts. Cuts were made, the list trimmed to 32 players, who then moved into Assembly Hall to play doubleheaders on April 21 and April 22, in front of live crowds rather than the NBA scouts and media who had watched the earlier goings-on. Among the players who had been cut by now were future NBA pros Kenny Walker, Mark Price and Michael Cage.

Knight climbed down from his tower to more closely inspect the remaining players.

Over the next weeks, the squad would be trimmed from 32 to 20 and then to 16 by May. Gone were future NBA pros Karl Malone and Antoine Carr, who had been playing abroad, in an Italian league.

Knight's final cuts produced this 12-man squad: Forwards Sam Perkins (North Carolina), Wayman Tisdale (Oklahoma) and Jeff Turner (Vanderbilt) ; centers Patrick Ewing (Georgetown), Jon Koncak (SMU) and Joe Kleine (Arkansas); guards Michael Jordan (North Carolina), Chris Mullin (St. John's), Alvin Robertson (Arkansas), Steve Alford (Indiana), Leon Wood (Cal State-Fullerton) and Vern Fleming (Georgia).

Among those players who just missed making the team were future pros John Stockton, Terry Porter, Chuck Person and—the most controversial cut—Charles Barkley.

Early on, Barkley had dominated his peers, powering his way to the basket, executing soaring dunks that a working knowledge of physics said a man of his 284 pounds shouldn't be able to do.

"Barkley's like something off the pad at Canaveral," said Al Menendez, director of player personnel for the New Jersey Nets. "He flies through the air and you don't know how."

So what happened? Well, Sir Charles, as he came to be known, was not out of the Chip Hilton mold that Coach preferred. He was an individualist on and off the court—and a bit of a wise guy. To put a fine point on it, he annoyed hell out of Knight, and for Barkley the feeling was mutual.

That antagonism was hidden at first. When cut, Barkley uttered platitudes about why Knight had not kept him—couldn't adapt to this on offense, or do that on defense. But some time later, reporter Mark Heisler of the *Los Angeles Times* quoted Barkley as saying he had a love-hate relationship with Knight: "I love to hate him."

Alvin Robertson told Heisler: "Charles didn't like anything about Coach Knight. There were a lot of confrontations with Knight. [The coaches] would talk about being on time. [Knight] was telling us all to be punctual and then he showed up about 10 minutes late. Charles got up and said, 'It's 10 after 5, where the hell have you been?' And Knight just went off—'Let me tell you something, you fat son of a bitch. There's only one leader in this army.' He just went totally nuts."

Leon Wood: "Charles' whole idea was to make the top five in the [NBA] draft. So he kicked butt. To me, he was the best player the first week. After his stock went up and it was known he was going to be in the top five, he pretty much coasted. I don't think he really wanted to play."

Knight had the players he wanted, and soon was working them with his in-your-face style. It was culture shock for some of these stars, who had played for more easy-going college coaches. Certain players found themselves regularly marked for Coach's angry rebukes: Tisdale. Alford. Wood. Turner.

Just as he did at Indiana, he harangued his Olympians, used profanity, tossed them out of practice. When Tisdale took a charge during a scrimmage—an uncharacteristic show of defensive grit, by Knight's view—the coach gave Tisdale a magic marker so that the player could sign his name on that piece of the court to memorialize the moment.

But Knight also had a fierce feeling for what Coach and his players were striving for—a feeling rooted in a patriotism he was not shy about sharing with his players. He gave each of the players a three-by-five photo of an Olympic gold medal and told them, "I want this in your pocket, whatever you have on, where you go, until the real thing is yours."

Later, when the team trained in San Diego, Knight introduced Alex Groza to his players. Groza had played for Kentucky's NCAA champions in 1948 and 1949 but had a thriving NBA career interrupted when he was implicated in a point-fixing college basketball scandal that shocked America in the early 50s.

But that was not why Knight asked Groza to attend a team practice. In addition to having played for Kentucky and for the NBA Indianapolis Olympians, Groza had been a member of the gold-medal U.S. basketball team at the 1948 Olympics. Groza had taken his gold medal and made it into a necklace for his wife. Knight asked him to bring the gold medal with him and had each player hold it.

"I could just see it in their faces," said Knight. "Each kid was reluctant to pass it onto the next kid, till all 12 of them had held that gold medal."

Through practices, through a series of exhibitions against a team of volunteer NBA stars—all nine games won by the Olympians—Knight drove his players. It was basketball boot camp, with Knight the drill instructor from hell. During games, he railed at mistakes and ranted at the officials, even incurring a technical and having to be restrained from going after one of the tooters

during an exhibition game. He never seemed satisfied. But the team was coming together. Players
were finding their roles. Wood was the point
guard. Mullin and Alford were the zone-
busters—both were deadly accurate jump shooters. Jordan was Jordan—a force at either end of
the court. Robertson was a hellacious defender.
Perkins was Knight's kind of sacrificer—a player
who worked hard and made his teammates better.
Tisdale and Ewing were the big men.

But even as they gelled as a unit, Knight kept
at them. Wood dribbled too much. Alford, who
would be going into his sophomore year at Indiana, needed to get after it on defense. Jordan—
please set a pick for somebody. And Ewing—
well, Ewing confounded Knight. Knight wanted
him to hound his opposite on defense rather than
sagging to the middle, but Ewing resisted, and
Knight finally told his assistants: "One of you
guys go coach the son of a bitch because I can't."
Four years later, Knight would say to Esquire's
Mike Lupica: "I don't think anybody will ever be
able to coach him."

Meanwhile, his players did their damnedest to
avoid his wrath. The experience of playing for
Bobby Knight was an unsettling one.

Tisdale: "The first time I saw him blow up
was at the second trials. He blew up, and I called

home that night and said, 'W-a-i-t a minute!' I didn't know what to think. . . . When I get back to Oklahoma, I'm going back there and hug every mean person that I used to think was mean. . . . I'm going to have a lot of respect for Steve Alford. He's got three more years of this."

Wood: "I saw Indiana play UCLA, and I saw him get all over Scott May, who was the Player of the Year. I was maybe 14 years old and I thought, 'God, this guy is a maniac. . . .' But I'd never met him. I just had to go from what I'd read. It's true, what I read."

Jordan: "Four years with him? I'd have to think about that for a while."

Turner: "I have a lot of respect for Steve Alford."

In 1980, prodded by President Jimmy Carter, the United States had boycotted the Moscow Olympics because the Russians were warring against Afghanistan.

In 1984, well after Knight had selected his team, the Russians returned the favor, saying no Soviet team would show up in Los Angeles.

That took some of the luster off the basketball competition, but publicly Knight would say—that it doesn't matter, those Reds can't play defense and there are plenty teams we'll face who are way better than the Ruskies anyhow.

"I don't think I have ever gone into anything with this degree of apprehension," Knight said, "because I want us to represent the United States so well."

Knight made it sound as though his talent-laden squad was in for a tough time—the hell with what those experts were saying. Like Blackie Sherrod of the *Dallas Times Herald,* who wrote:

Aw, come off it, Bobby Knight. . . . You are not walking through the valley of the shadow of death. You will win the Olympic basketball gold medal from here to Halifax, so quit biting your fingernails and pacing the floor.

In fact, the U.S. team was far superior to the competition. On July 29, 1984, the Americans opened their gold-medal drive by trouncing China, 97–49. Knight said afterward that hearing the partisan American crowd chant "USA, USA" was, in his term, "a hair-raising experience."

So it went. The United States pounded teams from Canada (89–68), Uruguay (104–68), France (120–62), and Spain (101–68). Jordan soared.

Ewing swatted. Mullin and Alford shot zones to pieces.

The only unpredictable twist in all this was how Knight would interact afterward at news conferences in which his remarks were translated into French by Marie Holgado, a pretty 26-year-old Parisian emigré. (Olympic protocol mandated that all media questions and answers be translated into French.) Knight sought to embarrass Holgado by injecting the word "ass" into his remarks. But the aspiring actress was undaunted and let Knight know it. He liked her feistiness. Soon he was bringing her gifts—flowers, candy, a dictionary, clacking plastic teeth—while the press hummed the theme from the French film *A Man and a Woman* and Holgado said of Coach, "Nice man, big mouth."

Next up was West Germany. The final score, 78–67, gave the illusion that the Germans had been competitive. The truth was that they had closed a 22-point gap to 11 during garbage time, angering Knight, who muttered: "I can't believe this team! I can't believe this team! They just go out and play the kind of game they want to play!"

The victory over West Germany put the Americans into the medal round, and a 78–59 win over Canada sent them into the gold-medal game against previously beaten Spain on August 10.

Spain proved no more difficult the second time around, although Knight acted as though the Americans were under siege. He kicked a water bottle after the U.S. lead reached 25 and then whoofed at Wood on the way into the lockerroom at the half.

The U.S. won the gold medal, beating Spain 96–65, with Jordan scoring a game-high 24 points.

Through eight games the U.S. had won by a margin of 32.1 points. Alford, whose selection to the team had been questioned by some critics, made 64 percent of his shots during the Olympics, including five of six in the gold-medal game.

After the players received their gold medals, on cue from Knight they carried Hank Iba off the floor—a gesture meant to allay the stigma of '72 and the criticism the old coach had gotten. Knight was teary-eyed as Iba was held aloft.

Afterward, Knight would try his best to prevent the absence of the Soviet Union from diminishing what Team USA had wrought.

"I've watched them [the Russians] play for two years," Knight told newsmen, "and we beat the Russians' butts anywhere they want to play. The Russians can't play defense. You tell me the Russians can play these guys. There is no way the Russians come close to this bunch."

Whatever. It was over. The U.S. had gold, and Knight had satisfaction, sort of. For as Paul Attner of the *Sporting News* would observe:

> Knight certainly won this medal his way—no modification in behavior, no peace with the press, no apparent enjoyment in what he was creating. It's too bad, because his genius should be hailed.

13

The Chair Rests

When the Olympics ended, C. M. Newton, the Vanderbilt coach who had served as team manager for U.S. basketball, suggested that his friend Bobby Knight take a sabbatical. University professors did it all the time—a year off to do research and/or re-charge their batteries. Why not a coach trying the same?

Newton's idea was well-intended. He believed Knight had driven himself so hard through the months leading up to Olympic gold that he was running near empty. It is speculation to say that Newton foresaw that a Bobby Knight in that condition was susceptible to the sort of impulsive misbehavior that had gotten him in jams before. But certainly the logic inherent in the very idea of a sabbatical tilted in that direction.

Knight declined to take time off. Since winning the NCAA championship in 1981, I-U teams had gone 19–10 ('81–82), 24–6 and a Big Ten title ('82–83) and a 22–9 season ('83–84) in which the Hoosiers had come within seconds of making it to the Final Four .

Off that '83–84 season, Indiana appeared to be one of the elite quintets as the new campaign loomed . In its 1984–85 college basketball preview issue, *Sports Illustrated* rated Indiana as the fifth-best team in America even as it noted the shaky co-existence between Knight and his seven-foot-two starting center, Uwe Blab, who was from Munich, West Germany:

> The relationship between Knight and Blab has always been one of Sturm und Drang. Blab has described playing for Knight as "hell" and once gave his coach the finger in full view of some 10,000 fans at Michigan State.

Nineteen eighty-four/eighty-five would see a whole lot of Sturm und Drang at I-U. It was a winter of discontent for Coach, who seemed to be perpetually dissatisfied with his players' effort, his anger hitting seismic heights. The team's leading rebounder, six-foot-nine sophomore Mike

Giomi, and six-foot-five junior swingman Winston Morgan bore the brunt of Knight's tirades, and Alford—who had performed so well at the Olympics—caught hell too.

Blab would say: "Coach Knight tends to get on people all the time. He's very smart about it. He tends to get on people who can handle it, and this team has a lot of people that can't handle it."

On January 19, 1985, Indiana lost to Knight's alma mater, Ohio State, 86–84. With that defeat the Hoosiers' record was 11–4—not nearly good enough according to Knight, though it would have satisfied most coaches. Knight felt the game could have been won—that the defense, the pride of his system, had been wretched. The statistics bore Knight out. I-U had given up 51 points to the Buckeyes in the first half. Pinpointing Giomi and Morgan as the most culpable players, Knight wouldn't allow them to fly back to Bloomington with the rest of the team. Instead he stuck them on the smaller of two charter planes the team used when it flew.

When Indiana played its next game five days later, against Purdue, Giomi and Morgan were still in Coach's doghouse. Knight wouldn't permit them to ride the team bus to Lafayette, forcing them instead to go by car with the team's physician, Dr. Brad Bomba.

Against archrival Purdue, with Giomi and Morgan benched for the whole game, Indiana blew a big lead in losing 62–52. Knight was enraged by what he perceived as lack of effort by his starters, and decided on a highly unorthodox way to send that message.

The team's next game was on January 27 against Illinois in Champaign. Knight decided he would leave Giomi and Morgan back in Bloomington and start Blab and four inexperienced freshmen—Delray Brooks, Steve Eyl, Joe Hillman and Brian Sloan. Through a first half that saw that aggregate five shoot 28 percent and score only 12 points, Knight stuck with his unlikely lineup. When he deigned to use substitutes, he turned to other sparingly used freshmen. The regulars? They never got off the bench as Indiana lost 52–41.

Knight's strategy enraged Hoosier fans, who saw him as giving away the game to perversely make a point. That Knight had sat Alford—an Indiana icon since his schoolboy days at New Castle High—was more than the rabid I-U supporters could bear. Even Knight's mother, Hazel, questioned him on that. Benching Steve Alford? What was Coach thinking? For the first time in his career, Bobby Knight was being ripped by I-U loyalists for his coaching.

The Illinois strategy was, predictably, a *cause célèbre* with the media. Wrote Frederick Klein in the *Wall Street Journal:*

> Any other coach of an 11–5 team with a shot at a conference title who benched four starters for a big game (and a TV game at that) would have been fired, institutionalized, or both. But Knight is beyond that. He has always been the guy who made the rules, not followed them.

The *New York Post* dispatched a reporter, Dave Hanson, to Bloomington to gauge the locals' mood. In a story headlined "Bad Bobby Sets Indiana on Fire," Bob Zaltsberg, managing editor of the *Bloomington Herald-Telephone*, was quoted as saying of Knight: "I don't think he's out of character at all. I just think he's taking his character to a new level. There are a lot of people in town who think he threw the game to make a point. The question is: what point?"

Knight's somewhat cryptic explanation was: "I think there comes a time that somebody needs to be jolted a little."

More jolting followed. Two days after the Illinois debacle, Knight threw Giomi off the team. At the time, Giomi was averaging 9.5 points per game and 5.3 rebounds a game. Knight claimed that Giomi had cut several classes, and by the coach's strict standards that was grounds for dismissal. But Giomi's mother, Karen, said her son—who at the time had a passable 2.4 academic average—was being scapegoated for the team's misfortunes. "Every year," she said, "Coach Knight picks out a player who is going to take the most abuse, and this year it's been Michael."

Whatever. Giomi, who would eventually transfer to North Carolina State, was gone, and it changed nothing. Even with its starters back in the lineup, Indiana continued to lose, getting trounced by Iowa in its next game, 72–59, for its fourth consecutive loss. In the stands, Knight's supporters and critics stated their positions. HEY BOB! WHY NOT START THE CHEERLEADERS? was the needling question the doubters asked. But Knight loyalists raised a sign that read: DO NOT QUESTION BOBBY.

Nearly a month later, on February 23, the Hoosiers were in the midst of another losing streak. Early in a game against Purdue, with Indiana trailing 11–2, Alford was assessed a foul during a scramble for a loose ball. As Purdue in-bounded the ball, another Hoosier, Daryl Thomas, was called for a personal foul. Knight blew up, cursing the referee, who immediately hit the coach with a technical foul.

As Purdue guard Steve Reid stepped to the foul line by the Indiana bench, in readiness to shoot the technical, Knight reached down for the orange plastic chair on which he'd been sitting. He grabbed the chair with both hands and side-armed it across the floor. The chair skidded along the floor, past Reid, and came to rest at the far side of the court.

Knight had done it again. He had erupted, providing an apocalyptic moment for those who viewed him as a Knightmare. The filmed footage of the chair throw would follow Knight—yea, haunt him—through the years. After that game, whenever Coach created a scene, had an incident, blew up, and your TV sportscaster wanted to set it in context, sure as hell that chair fling would be replayed. It would be an affirming moment for anyone positing the notion that Knight was a nut job.

Knight knew that even for Bobby Knight he'd crossed the line. There were tears in his eyes when Indiana's president, John Ryan, a long-time ally, encountered him in the Hoosier dressing room, where Knight had been banished by the officials after incurring two more technicals for his chair throw.

"Dr. Ryan," said Knight, "I'm sorry."

With Knight gone, Indiana suffered its third straight loss, Purdue beating the Hoosiers 72–63.

In a statement conveyed through the Indiana sport information office, Knight issued this public apology:

> While I have been very concerned of the way some things have been handled in the Big Ten, in particular the officiating which has really frustrated me the past couple of years, I do not think my action in the Purdue game was in any way necessary or appropriate. No one realizes that more than I do.
>
> I am certain that what I did in tossing the chair was an embarrassment to Indiana University. That was not my intention and for that reason I'm deeply sorry for it. The personal support I have had from Indiana University and its fans has been tremendous, and to have an incident like this cause them real concern bothers me.
>
> While I certainly take exception to criticism on who I start or play in any game, I feel a criticism of my action in throwing the chair is justifiable. It's something that I will not let happen again.

The irony here was that during a practice Knight had once been so angered that he'd picked up and thrown thirteen chairs, one after another, around the gym. But of course it was one thing to go ballistic behind those black curtains at a Hoosiers' practice and quite another to lose control in public.

Knight's chair toss inspired John Perazzo, general manager of the 52nd Street Pub and Ale House in Indianapolis, to stage a chair-throwing contest in his establishment's parking lot. Perazzo took out an ad in the *Indianapolis Star*, inviting one and all to loft a folding chair painted white with red I-U letters at another chair painted black and white to represent a referee. Twenty-five contestants competed, and two local TV sportscasters, Jim Barber and Lee Owens, and a third man who was a friend of Perazzo's acted as the judges. Contestants were judged on accuracy and style. The winner of the $100 prize, Craig Church, darted from the crowd with the throwing chair, did a somersault with it and then hit the target chair at a distance of 20 yards.

In other circles, Knight's behavior inspired more severe reactions. Dean Hock of Elkhart, a member of the Indiana House of Representatives, filed a motion seeking censure of Knight. Hock said that when he played high school basketball "it was always drilled into me that it's not whether you win or lose but how you play the game."

Hock went on to say, "We can't condone stuff like that in a state-supported university that's supposed to be a model for our young people. It's bad enough in professional sports where there's big money involved.

"If he's always been that way, he should get out of coaching. If the pressures have caused him to lose his cool, then he should take some time off."

Meanwhile, at Vanderbilt, C. M. Newton, who had proposed that sabbatical for Knight, now told newsmen: "There's no doubt in my mind that what you're seeing now is tied in with that [Olympic] experience. No one, unless you've been through it, realizes how intense the whole Olympic experience was."

George Raveling, who had been one of Knight's assistants during the Olympics, quipped: "The good thing about it is there are only four [regular-season] games left."

Actually, three for Knight. He was suspended for one game by Wayne Duke, the Big Ten commissioner, for the chair toss. On March 3, with Knight sitting out the game and assistant coach Jim Crews taking his place, Indiana lost to Iowa, 70–50, its fourth loss in five games.

As seasons go, this one had, as Alford would say, "a black cloud" over it, even with the Hoosiers winning four games in the NIT and landing in the finals against UCLA. That prompted TV's Bill Raftery to ask Knight what he liked best about the way his team had played in the NIT. "What I like best about this team right now," Knight said, "is the fact that I only have to watch it play one more time."

UCLA beat Indiana 65–62, the Hoosiers finishing their troubled season with a 19–14 record.

A little more than a month later, at a dinner honoring his old Ohio State coach, Fred Taylor, Knight told the audience: "I've been asked to do a number of clinics and such lately. But I just had to tell them all that I'm getting out of coaching. That's right. I'm going into the furniture business. In fact, I've already told prospective customers that after I open the store, when anybody buys a sofa, I'll throw in a chair."

14

Good Bobby, Bad Bobby

"KNIGHT HOPES A BOOK WILL IM-
PROVE HIS IMAGE."

That was the headline on the sports page of
the *Los Angeles Times* in the midst of a new
season.

Nineteen eighty-five/eighty six was underway
and Bobby Knight—that sworn enemy and perpetual critic of the press—had, improbable as it
was, granted a writer full access to his operation.

It was, as the *Wall Street Journal*'s Frederick
Klein noted, "astonishing because Knight usually
regards journalists as he would a collection of
dead fish that hasn't been properly refrigerated."

But unlikely as it seemed, John Feinstein of
the *Washington Post* was on the job. He had been
greenlighted by Knight to track the daily events,

large and small, of the Hoosiers' season—from
the first day of practice to the shocking loss in
the first round of the NCAAs to upstart Cleveland
State.

While following Knight, Feinstein lived in an
off-campus student apartment, five minutes from
Assembly Hall. He attended each game and practice, kept a diary and tape-recorded what Knight
said to players and assistants.

By February of the '85–86 season, Feinstein
was telling reporters: "He hasn't barred me from
anything—practices, meetings, planes, hotel
rooms, the dressing room before, during and after
games. I don't see how an outsider could get
closer to a basketball team."

It's hard to imagine what Knight expected the
result to be of his giving a top-flight journalist
like Feinstein an up-close, personal look at his
complex character.

"Bobby believes, naturally, that he's a good
guy," said Feinstein during the season. "I think
he feels that if people are permitted to see him,
warts and all, they'll have a better understanding
of him and how he acts. He cares about the kids
so much that if they spend four years with him,
he feels he owes them something. He's a decent
fellow, a good guy.

"But the book will contain things he won't

like. When he protests, I hope his friends will say, 'Yes, Bobby, you really are that way sometimes."

Or, as Feinstein wrote to a friend during the Hoosiers' chaotic 21–8 season: "Bobby Knight is the best guy I've ever met; Bobby Knight is the worst guy I've ever met."

The facts that Feinstein laid out in *A Season on the Brink: A Year with Bob Knight and the Indiana Hoosiers* showed the coach in full. But even with Feinstein giving Knight his due as a dedicated coach and a loyal friend, it wasn't a pretty picture.

As the *Wall Street Journal*'s Klein would say in his review of the book:

> The good stuff . . . doesn't nearly off-set Mr. Feinstein's vivid portrait of Knight's dark side. We see Knight as a bully who takes the floor in practice to impress his charges with his ballhandling prowess and throws a ball in the face of a player who had the audacity to steal one of his passes. . . .
>
> Knight displays a vocabulary of profanity that would shock a teamster, and he is not loath to use it on his players. He plays unremitting "mind games" with his team, ripping it verbally, dismissing it

from practice, calling it back and dismissing it again with threat to terminate the season. Sometimes there's an encouraging word to offset the abuse, and sometimes no.

On the '85–86 Indiana team, a six-foot-seven junior named Daryl Thomas was a frequent target of Knight's displeasure. Thomas was a starter who would average 14.5 ppg during the year, yet rarely satisfy his coach's expectations. The recurring theme in Knight's denunciations of Thomas was that he played "soft"—a point he regularly voiced to the player.

Years later, when the CNN/SI segment prompted folks who had experienced the dark side of Bobby Knight to go public, one former I-U player who stepped forward to defend the coach was Joe Hillman. Hillman, who was a freshman in '85–86, viewed Knight as a demanding coach whose discipline ultimately strengthened his charges—made men of them, so to speak.

Hillman illustrated his point when he told reporters from the Indianapolis Star how Knight in one instance had dealt with Thomas's perceived passivity. "Now he was after Daryl good," said Hillman. "We needed Daryl to play a lot tougher than he was playing. And Knight was pushing him, and grinding him, and he got after him. He said, 'Now dammit, Daryl, I want you to hit me. I want you to smack me, Daryl. We need to make you a man, Daryl.' "

Thomas, Hillman recalled, "just sat there; he didn't do anything. And so Knight whacked him upside of the head."

According to Hillman, Knight then asked Thomas to hit him back. When Thomas did so, the coach was pleased.

Said Hillman of Knight's open-handed slap, "It wasn't a hit in anger. It wasn't a violent act."

To outsiders—those who had played the game and those who merely enjoyed watching it—this supposed shining example of Knight's tough love may have seemed excessive—may, in fact, have struck a civilian as reprehensible. It depended on one's perspective on discipline/coaches/life. But by the year 2000, when Hillman mentioned the anecdote, it was but one of many strange tales being told about a coach suddenly being looked upon with suspicion.

When Feinstein's *A Season on the Brink* was published in 1986, the Knight he exposed stood out more starkly at the time. Even though Knight had been criticized by sportswriters before, the depth of Feinstein's research made for a "revealing" portrait: Come see the crazy bastard who coaches I-U—step this way—the $16.95 price of the book gets you inside Hoosier basketball, right down there on the Assembly Hall practice floor that I-U players, in a display of gallows humor, referred to as "Monroe County Jail."

Take Daryl Thomas. Feinstein showed in vivid detail what Thomas, characterized by the author as a sensitive sort, endured of Knight's abuse during a single day's practice:

First, he screamed at Thomas for playing carelessly. Then, he banished him from the scrimmage, sending him to a lone basket at the end of the court to practice with Magnus Pelkowski, a 6-foot-10 sophomore who was not scrimmaging because of an injury.

"Daryl," he screamed as Thomas walked toward where Pelkowski was working, "get the f— out of my sight. If that's the best you can give us after two days rest, get away from me. There is absolutely no way you'll start on Saturday. No way. You cost yourself that chance today by f— around. You are so terrible, it's just awful. I don't know what the f— you are thinking about. You think I was

mad last year? You saw me, I was the mad-
dest sonofabitch you ever saw. You want
another year like that? Just get the f— out
of my sight."

As Thomas was dismissed from practice,
Knight trashed him to his assistants ("Fuck Daryl
Thomas"). Then, when Thomas rejoined the
squad to review a tape of the day's practice, the
coach lit into him again. He called Thomas "a
fucking joke" and then provided supporting data
from his critique of the tape:

"Look at that! You are the worst f—
pussy I've ever seen play basketball at this
school. . . . You have more goddamn ability than 95 percent of the players we've
had here but you're are a pussy from the
top of your head to the bottom of your
feet. An absolute f— pussy."

By Feinstein's account, Thomas was fighting
back tears. And later, when Knight—realizing he
had been too brutal—sent an assistant coach to
comfort him, Thomas cried. Wrote Feinstein:

Thomas was facing the same question
everyone who comes in contact with

Knight faces sooner or later: Is it worth it? Does the end justify the means? He knew Knight just wanted him to be a better player. He knew Knight liked him and cared about him. He knew that if anyone ever attacked him, Knight would come to his defense. But was all that worth it for this? This was Knight at his meanest.

A Season on the Brink became a best-seller—and a sore point for Knight. He claimed Feinstein had sandbagged him by telling him the focus of the book would be on the players, not the coach, and by promising to clean up his language. Feinstein denied making any such promises. The feud didn't hurt sales of the book any.

Since his success at the Olympics, Knight's image had taken hits. There had been one controversy after another. The furor surrounding his use of the four freshmen against Illinois. The chair fling. The Giomi dismissal. He'd even responded to the obscene insults of Purdue fans by bringing a donkey onto the set of his TV show and telling viewers the creature was a Purdue man.

Then—John Feinstein's revealing portrait.

Yet a year later (1986–87), like him or not, here was Bobby Knight with another Hoosier team ready to challenge for his third NCAA title.

As Bobby Knight's NCAA contenders went, the 1986–87 bunch hadn't the conspicuous NBA-level talent that his previous national champions did.

Alford, a senior now, was as good a pure shooter as Knight had had. In his four seasons in Bloomington, Alford had led the team every year in scoring, averaging 22 points per game as a senior. But Alford's skills, it turned out, didn't compute as a pro. He played three seasons at Golden State and Dallas, averaging 4.4 ppg, and then turned to coaching.

On Knight's '86–87 team were a pair of junior college players, a species the coach rarely recruited. But both Keith Smart, a six-foot-one junior guard from Garden City (Kansas) Community College and Dean Garrett, a six-foot-ten junior center from San Francisco City College, would be starters for Knight '86–87 squad.

Smart would have a short-lived NBA fling— two games (a one point per game average) with San Antonio before being let go. He went on to play abroad and in American minor leagues for several years before becoming coach of the Continental Basketball Association Fort Wayne Fury.

Garrett was selected in the second round of the 1988 NBA draft by the Phoenix Suns, but chose instead to play abroad. From 1988 to 1996, he drew wages from Italian and Greek teams. In 1996, he returned to the States as a late-blooming NBA player: four seasons with Minnesota and Detroit that saw him average 6 point per game and 6 rebounds a game.

Unlike Knight's blessed '75–76 squad, this team hadn't the expectations that the Buckner-May-Benson aggregate did. But under Knight the team developed a chemistry that, by God, proved better than the experts or even Coach figured. It was Bobby Knight basketball—the death-before-dishonor man-to-man defense and the patient passing game whose elements Knight had first glimpsed when Butch van Breda Kolff was coaching it at Princeton. The lineup featured Alford, Smart, Garrett, six-foot-six sophomore Ricky Calloway and the often-abused Daryl Thomas, now a senior.

Indiana went 24–4 during the regular season, earning a share of the Big Ten title. But while the Hoosiers had ended up number 2 in the UPI's coaches poll and number 3 in the Associated Press media poll, they were not projected as any sort of runaway favorite in the NCAA tournament's 64-team field.

But game by game, Indiana did what it had to—it blew out underdog Fairfield 92–58, rallied from a 24–10 deficit against Auburn behind Alford's 31 points to win 107–90, edged a Duke team coached by a Knight player from Army, Mike Krzyzewski, 88–82, and then staged a late rally against LSU, overcoming a nine-point deficit in the final five minutes to win 77–76.

During those hectic final minutes, Knight, who had incurred a technical earlier, railed at the game's officials over a call, emphasizing his displeasure by pounding his fist so hard against the scorer's table that a telephone on it jumped. LSU coach Dale Brown was outraged that the officials let Knight vent like that without assessing another technical foul. Afterward, Brown insisted that the officials had given latitude to Indiana's recklessly aggressive pressing defense down the stretch because Knight had intimidated them. Knight fired back that that wasn't the case at all—Brown had just coached lousy. A very public feud grew, Brown some time later challenging Knight to step into a locked room and mud-wrestle him.

Whatever. Indiana—fined $10,000 by the NCAA for Knight's fist-pounding—had made it to the Final Four in the New Orleans' Superdome. Knight had drawn a reprimand from the NCAA, but what did that mean to a college coach who had pushed, prodded and provoked his team into championship contention?

Jerry Tarkanian's freewheeling UNLV team

was next for the Hoosiers. The Running Rebels, the tournament favorite, were powered by the 3-point shoooting of Freddie Banks, and the inside game of Armon Gilliam. Banks bombed 10 of 19 three point shots in totalling 38 points, and Gilliam had 32 points, but Indiana was able to match the run-n-gun fervor of the Rebels. Alford scored 33 points in leading I-U to a 97–93 victory.

Meanwhile, Syracuse beat Providence 77–63 to set up an Indiana-Syracuse title game. Syracuse, a first-time finalist, had three future NBA players in Derrick Coleman, Rony Seikaly and Sherman Douglas. The Orangemen had entered the tournament a long-shot, but did better than analysts figured.

Against Indiana, before a Superdome crowd of 64,959, Syracuse proved good enough to take Indiana right down to the wire—good enough, in fact, to lead the Hoosiers 73–72 with 28 seconds remaining.

Knight drew up the final play so that Alford would get the shot. But Xs and Os don't always shake out the way coaches design them. In the hurly burly of those final moments, his teammates could not get the ball to Alford. In the end, the ball game would ride on Keith Smart, who'd grown up just down the road in Baton Rouge, where he'd been a fry cook at McDonald's after graduating from high school.

Ironically, Smart had been benched earlier in the second half for an errant pass and then sent back in with Knight's warning that he had better produce or could count on being returned to the pine.

Smart heated up. Syracuse, which held a 5-point lead with 7:22 left in the game, couldn't stop Smart's leaping bank shots and layups. As Indiana emerged from its final huddle, expecting to get the ball in Alford's hand, Smart had scored 13 second-half points, 19 in all.

But his next shot, a 16-foot jumper from the corner with the game clock running down would, like Bobby Plump's game winner for Milan High, become Hoosier lore. Smart's shot dropped cleanly through the hoop with five seconds left. Syracuse's Coleman threw a long pass downcourt, but Smart intercepted. Ball game! Indiana 74, Syracuse 73.

For Bobby Knight, it marked his third NCAA champion. He didn't know it then, but that glory would not be revisited by Coach in the years leading to the new millennium. Just the same, they would not be dull years. Not with Bobby Knight, a man ever on the brink of another controversy.

15

Tick, Tick, Tick

It had not been a good day for Fred Nichols, dean of students at Wilfred Laurier University in Waterloo, Ontario. But what could that possibly have to do with Bobby Knight?

In a letter to *Sports Illustrated,* Nichols, responding to critical reportage on Knight, told how while he was parked at a service station near Mobile, Ala., on April 1, 1987, a trucker lost his brakes and totalled Nichols' car while severely injuring the dean's wife. Nichols felt utter despair until a stranger put his hand on his shoulder and began to reassure him:

> I looked at him and said, "You look like Bobby Knight." He said, "I am, but we won't talk about that right now."

Knight, who was fresh from the NCAA championship in New Orleans and en route to Atlanta to receive the Tipoff's Club's Naismith Coach of the Year Award, proceeded to take charge of the accident scene.

Perhaps somebody else would have done the same thing, but somebody else did not. Knight did, and he did it without any of the headlines or acclaim he had received just two nights earlier when his Hoosiers won the NCAA tournament.

I'm told that after my wife and I left the scene by ambulance, Knight stayed with our automobile to protect our personal belongings until the wreckers arrived.

The story is a touching one, reflecting favorably on Knight. What he did at the roadside gas station was a noble act. Those who knew him well would tell you it was not an isolated instance of Coach's capacity to reach out to others. Bobby Knight was a bright man, often funny, with a strong sense of values.

Yet over the next thirteeen years, following the NCAA title win in New Orleans, he was frequently his own worst enemy, behaving in ways that mystified even those closest friends. The incidents in which he became embroiled began to define him more and more as the ticking time bomb that so many folks—those near to him or watching from a respectful distance—saw him as. More so as his success as a coach diminished. Not that Indiana teams weren't competitive after '86–87. They were, but they hadn't the spark of past Hoosier teams. Indiana repeatedly failed in the postseason. At NCAA time, I-U routinely got bounced early from the tournament, many observers insisting that the players appeared too tightly-wound—unnerved, it seemed, by their tightly-wound coach.

Questions would be raised about whether Knight was out of step with the sort of self-absorbed athletes emerging from high schools. That 50s paradigm, Chip Hilton, was no more. The age of me-first hoopsters had arrived—a species at odds with Knight's fundamentalist approach to the game.

Down the road to the new millennium life got complicated for Bobby Knight.

He never backed into a thought. Never equivocated. Bobby Knight said what was on his mind. He was as subtle as a steam shovel. He had his opinions and, frankly, didn't give a damn whether you agreed or not.

The disciplined approach he brought to the game of basketball was reflected in how he saw life. Knight's version ran something like this: You reap what you sow. Work hard, keep to the straight and narrow—and success is within range. Tinker with that ethic, you risk a misstep. And when that happens, too bad—you've screwed up. Losers weepers.

So when Len Bias, the University of Maryland star who was the Boston Celtics' top draft choice in 1986, celebrated his upcoming big-money contract with cocaine, and ended up dead from it, Knight didn't go bleeding heart over what many saw as a tragedy.

Speaking to a group of blue-chip high school players at Howard Garfinkel's Five Star basketball camp, he said: "I don't feel sorry for Len Bias, not in the slightest. He had his own mind and his own body to take care of and just wasn't smart enough to do it.

"Those of you who have been popping pills and smoking dope are doing the same thing Len Bias did. Those are serious bad shots you're taking, boys, serious poor judgments that you're using with your body and mind. Len Bias was better than anybody here. . . . The only college

player I've seen in the past few years as good as
Bias was Michael Jordan, and I'm not sure if he
was as good as Bias was in college, and Bias is
dead.

"He's dead because he just wasn't strong
enough to take care of himself. Somewhere along
the way he wanted to be one of the boys. He
wanted to be cool. Well, he was so cool that he's
cold right now. . . . That's how cool he was."

Hard work. No screwing around. It was how
Knight went about his business. The anger that
fueled Knight—that temper that he'd shown
going back to Orrville—was by now part of his
public image. Almost a trademark. Like Sinatra
had a temper, so did Coach. No big deal. In Indiana, folks were inclined to think of it as a quirk.

Stories abounded about Knight's temper, and
were told with a kind of relish by his admirers.
Some of the tales may have even been apocry-
phal. Didn't matter. Enough of them were for-
sure true that a little elaboration here or there—
what harm? Those who revered Coach told these
anecdotes with a kind of good-ole-boy affection.
Damn. That Bobby. They made him out the
Moby Dick of soreheads.

There was the tale told of the time he broke
one golf club after another during a round of
poorly executed shots. As his bag of available

clubs thinned out to a precious few, Knight finally smashed a drive straight and true down the fairway, prompting a partner to quip: "All I can say is that that club was really fighting for its life."

A quirk. That's what the outbursts represented to Knight loyalists. But the larger picture was that Coach had been too long condoned, and no limits existed. The temper was part of an autocratic personality that saw him say what he wanted and do what he wanted, and not worry about consequences. Consequences? Hey, he was Bobby Knight, wasn't he?

There was an air of disdain for those who didn't meet his expectations, or view him as sympathetically as he wanted. And he didn't mind letting them know, didn't mind messing with their heads. Once, when a reporter wondered whether the Hoosiers' reduction of turnovers in the second half was the result of their getting acclimated to a hostile crowd, Knight responded: "Well, I think the oxygen content is lower here than in Bloomington. And when you have low oxygen content, the ball travels faster. I just think that the ball was traveling too fast for us in the first half. But I thought we adjusted well to the sparse oxygen in the second half."

Yup, he was Bobby Knight. He could do and say what he wanted.

In November 1987, Knight pulled his team off the floor with 15 minutes left to play in an exhibition game against a team from the USSR after being ejected for arguing a referee's call.

At the time, Indiana University had a new president, Thomas Ehrlich. For sixteen years, Ehrlich's predecessor, John Ryan, had taken a laissez-faire attitude toward Knight's excesses. When Knight screwed up, Ryan looked the other way. The notorious chair toss? Ryan had let Big Ten commissioner Wayne Duke suspend him rather than give Knight cause to think he wasn't beloved by the I-U administration. Whatever. Ehrlich, who had come onto the job in August, apparently didn't know Knight was not subject to criticism. He reprimanded Knight for yanking the team against the Russians.

Five months later, on April 25, 1988, Knight was interviewed for an NBC-TV special on "stress." Knight was asked by reporter Connie Chung, "There are times Bobby Knight can't do it his way—and what does he do then?"

Knight's response? "I think that if rape is inevitable, relax and enjoy it."

For years, in casual circumstances, among cronies, Knight had cracked wise about women. He'd been a Bloomington Archie Bunker. He liked to say that the only things women were good for were having kids and frying bacon. Insulting his players, he frequently maligned them as "pussies" and sometimes expanded on the theme. In *A Season on the Brink,* Feinstein had written: "Knight's sexism is no secret. In fact, he often wears it like a badge of honor."

Sports Illustrated's Rick Telander wrote:

> Knight has long displayed an insensitivity toward women, particularly those who invade his sacred basketball realm. He has ridiculed women reporters and has drawn obscene pictures when he knew they were watching.

To a reporter from *Indianapolis Monthly,* he had said that women waste too much time "talking about inconsequential things that wear my patience—'How are your children, how are you grandchildren?' Inconsequential. Too many housewives don't pay attention to what the hell's going on at home. I think women are housewives—a woman who is married and has a family is a housewife and mother before anything else. If she finds it boring, then goddammit, she shouldn't have kids."

In the circles in which he moved, that sort of sexist rant was viewed good-naturedly. You know. "That damn Bobby."

But here on NBC-TV, with the whole world watching, well—even Knight recognized that his response to Chung's question was inappropriate. In his next breath, he tried to mitigate his blunder, saying: "That's just an old term that you're going to use. The plane's down, so you have no control over it. I'm not talking about that, about the act of rape. Don't misinterpret me there. But what I'm talking about is, something happens to you, so you have to handle it—now. "

Knight would ask NBC not to run his segment, but how could the network resist a built-in controversy? And now Coach was stuck with the "rape" remark. Women's groups were incensed by his words and let the media know it. On the Indiana campus, rape was a reality. In 1986, a former I-U student living in Bloomington was raped and dismembered. I-U, with 32,500 students, had 12 reported rapes in 1987, and 6 rapes and 14 attempts since the beginning of 1988.

The campus switchboard logged 100 complaint calls over the next week and a campus rally drew 300 protestors carrying signs that read "Rape Is Every Woman's Knightmare" and "Rape Is No Game."

In politically correct times, sexist behavior and sexist language could kill a career. It had happened in New York City, where Tex Antoine, a veteran weatherman on the local ABC-TV newscast there, had made a remark similar to Knight's and was banished from the airwaves. In Madison, Wisconsin, a judge named Archie Simonson was recalled by voters after saying from the bench that a teenaged boy had reacted "normally" when he allegedly raped a co-ed.

While Knight's career was not jeopardized in the same way, he knew enough to offer an explanation. In an interview with Bob Hammel of the *Bloomington Herald-Telephone,* the coach said: "Anybody who knows me would be quick to say I would be one of the last people to adopt a careless attitude about rape as criminal assault, or toward any form of crime.

"The word *rape* can be used in several ways. One is in something that has gone out of control or over which you have no control. It obviously was in that context that I was using the word, as I explained in the interview."

Not good enough.

I-U president Erlich told the *New York Times*: "Coach Knight was not speaking for the university. His reference to rape and his coarse language were in very poor taste. Period. That's all I really want to say."

Trish Bracken, an assistant to the school's dean for women's affairs, said, "Coach Knight's stature as a role model and as an educator make it particularly dismaying. People who don't normally pay attention to sexist remarks are astounded. It's something you expect your grandfather to say. That a man with Coach Knight's education would say that is shocking."

Want "shocking," Hoosier fans?

Here it was. Hard on the controversy stirred up by Knight's use of the word *rape* with Connie Chung, Coach, it was said, was thinking of moving on—maybe taking over the basketball program at the University of New Mexico.

It was May 1988. Big headlines followed:

KNIGHT WEIGHS NEW MEXICO JOB OFFER

HOOSIERS LOSING KNIGHT?

FANS WAIT, HOPE KNIGHT WON'T GO

Knight, who frequently went fishing in New Mexico with former Lobo coach Norm Ellenberger, reportedly had asked Ellenberger whether the job was available. Ellenberger had put him in touch with the school's athletic director. Discussions had ensued.

Reports said that New Mexico was offering a five-year deal worth $250,000 to $300,000 annually in salary. That was quite a bit more than the reported $95,000 Indiana paid him, although that sum was supplemented heavily by income derived from outside sources—commercials, clinics, his TV and radio shows and a basketball shoe deal.

A *Dallas Times-Herald* story on May 12 quoted "sources close to Knight and the Lobos' program" as having reached an oral agreement with Knight and that it was "a done deal."

Knight, however, was not commenting, preferring to allow speculation to grow.

The *Chicago Tribune* wrote:

> Indiana had survived talk in the past that Knight was going to such places as Ohio State or CBS. But those who had been through it before said none of the past rumors had the urgency—and, they feared, the currency—of the new speculation that Knight is leaving. News reports quoted Knight as praising New Mexico and complaining about "changes" at the university, which many believed was a reference to President Thomas P. Ehrlich.

In fact, Ehrlich was the issue. And in his way, by allowing himself to be wooed by New Mexico, Knight was using the leverage he had as a coaching icon in Indiana to face down the bow-tie wearing Ehrlich. Bobby Knight was accustomed to being deferred to by the I-U administration— allowed to be all the Bobby Knight he wanted to be. Bad times, good times—you just patted Coach on the back of the red sweater he wore to games, a fashion change from the plaid jacket— and genuflected before the mention of his name.

As New Mexico explored their offer with Knight, sources close to Knight began letting reporters know how Coach felt about Ehrlich's taking him to task for the Chung interview and, before that, for pulling the team off the floor in the exhibition against the Russians.

Fred Taylor: "I think he feels like he's been abandoned at Indiana."

Billy Packer: "He's looking for new challenges and there's been a change of leadership at Indiana."

Dick Vitale: "Until this year, everyone in Indiana defended Bobby for his actions."

Pete Newell: "He truly feels he has a problem there [at Indiana] and he feels he can't get it resolved."

Bob Hammel: "Some of this is about the uncertainty to how the future looks for relations between the two. Nobody wants to have a battle every three months."

Before long, Knight was letting it be known that yes, he had a problem with Ehrlich, a magna cum laude graduate of Harvard and its law school, a man who had worked for Presidents Carter and Ford.

Knight told the *St. Petersburg* (Fla.) *Times*: "What really ticked me off is the president's deal. The president never talked with me. He didn't get my side. I really have a problem with that. Don't you build up some rights?"

Folks certainly thought so in Indiana. A rally in support of the coach was convened outside Assembly Hall, with an estimated 750 to 1,000 Knight loyalists showing up. Students carried placards reading SEND EHRLICH TO NEW MEXICO and V-NECKS, NOT BOW TIES a reference to Knight's red sweater and Ehrlich's favored neckwear.

Knight passed by the gathering crowd at one point but said nothing to his supporters or to the 20 reporters who followed him to his maroon Ford Bronco. As he drove away, several of his fans shouted, "We love you, Bobby . . . Don't leave."

At one point during the rally, about 80 of those pro-Knight demonstrators left and headed to Bryan House, Ehrlich's campus residence. On the chance that these students mean to stir up trouble, police cars were dispatched to the president's place.

Ehrlich was not happy at being depicted as Knight's boogey man. It was not a popular position to occupy in basketball-mad Indiana. So—

"In my view," said Ehrlich, "he's an outstanding coach and I certainly want him to stay."

On May 17, 1988, under the headline "KNIGHT DECIDES TO STAY WITH INDIANA," the *New York Times* noted:

> Knight's decision to honor a contract that runs until June 30, 1997, a decision he gave to his university president, Thomas Ehrlich, during a meeting Sunday night, ended one of the most tumultuous episodes of his controversial stay. Supporters in the two states produced alternating pep rallies and full-page newspaper advertisements in an effort to employ a coach whose Hoosier teams have won three national championships in his 17 seasons.

Ehrlich was quoted as saying: "I have come through the last week with a new appreciation of what it's like to be in the middle of a press blitz."

For the time being, the latest bit of fussing over Bobby Knight was over. Coach was back.

But that was never a guarantee that peace was at hand.

Tick, tick, tick.

The Ehrlich matter was a case study.

It showed how accustomed to having his way Knight had become—and how defensive he could be when a sober assessment was made about his behavior.

Stubborn. Prideful. Never wrong. Bobby Knight was Alpha male. He led, you followed. And when things got muddled, or complicated— just tell folks to shove it.

It was March 1992. Bobby Knight's Hoosiers were 23–6 and headed for the NCAAs. Knight's squad featured one senior, Eric Anderson, and five underclassmen: Alan Henderson (freshman), Damon Bailey (sophomore), and juniors Greg Graham, Chris Reynolds and leading scorer, Calbert Cheaney.

It was an incident with Cheaney that would again expose Knight's inability to engage a perspective larger than his own. It happened after Indiana had beaten its first three NCAA opponents—Eastern Illinois (94–55), Shaquille O'Neal's LSU (89–79), and Florida State (85–74)—and then headed to Albuquerque, New Mexico, to take on UCLA.

During a practice, Knight jokingly brandished a bullwhip that his players had given him. A photographer for the *Albuquerque Journal* caught the moment in which the bullwhip-wielding Knight stood poised over Cheaney, whose shorts were pulled down. Knight appeared to be on the verge of giving him a lick. Because Cheaney is a black man, the photo had disturbing associations for other blacks.

"It evokes images of the times when white men used to use a whip to keep black men and women in line," said Alice Hoppes, president of the Albuquerque chapter of the NAACP. "Those are images we would like to forget."

Cheaney defended his coach, saying that he took no offense at Knight's joke and, besides, Knight had pretended to "whip" a white player, Pat Graham, too. But when the subject of the bullwhip was raised with Knight after the Hoosiers beat UCLA 106–79, he cavalierly dismissed it, saying: "Don't even bother me with that shit. What I should apologize for is, I think, 18 black kids having played four years for me, with 15 of them having degrees. I recruited the first black kid to ever play at West Point. Those are the things I guess I need to apologize for."

A simple "sorry" would have quashed the matter. Nobody—not the NAACP's Hoppes or the coach's media critics—was making out Knight as a racist. As the *Boston Globe*'s Bob Ryan needled: "Anybody who knows, or who has studied Bob Knight knows, he is an equal opportunity abuser."

The issue here was sensitivity to others—that enlarged perspective that Coach's ego apparently couldn't countenance. So rather than putting an end to what most would regard as an inappropriate moment, Knight made his bad attitude the larger issue.

"He's insensitive and cannot understand what that message sends," said Hoppes. "We've got to learn from the past. People need to realize that a whip to an Afro-American is like a swastika to the Jews."

The leader of the Indiana General Assembly's black caucus was troubled enough by Knight's response to write I-U president Ehrlich, saying: "Serious consideration should be given to whether the best interests of Indiana University might not be better served if Mr. Knight's services were terminated."

But this time Ehrlich took a pass, declining comment on his coach's latest episode.

Knight? He showed up at a subsequent news conference with the whip and joked, "You don't mind if I prepare for practice while we talk, do you?"

Indiana's victory over UCLA sent the Hoosiers into the Final Four, with Duke their first opponent.

Duke was coached now by Mike Krzyzewski, whom Knight had regarded as the quintessential overachiever as a player.

Through the years, the two men had been close, Knight hiring Krzyzewski as an assistant at Indiana and then recommending him when the coaching job went vacant at Army. In 1986, when Duke reached its first Final Four under Krzyzewski, Knight had shown up at the tournament wearing a Blue Devil pin on his sweater. When Louisville upended Duke, Knight had called Krzyzewski the next week to console him.

So how to explain the brushoff Knight gave Coach K six years later, after Duke beat Knight's Hoosiers, 81–78, in the '91–92 Final Four? First, there was that quick handshake at final buzzer. Then, as the two men passed one another in the arena corridor 20 minutes later, no sign of recognition on Knight's part.

Bobby Knight had had spats with other coaches before-Joe B. Hall of Kentucky, Dale Brown of LSU, Bill Musselman of Minnesota. He'd criticized Lou Henson of Illinois for questionable recruiting practices. He'd ripped into Michigan's Bill Frieder after Frieder had encouraged an official to call a technical following an outburst by Knight. Those encounters had mostly occurred in the heat of battle.

But this split with Krzyzewski was more subtle. It seemed a case of the Alpha male feeling threatened. Had Knight gotten the notion that Krzyzewski had taken to minimizing Knight's impact on his career? A case of the acolyte getting big headed? Had he then written a letter to Coach K saying, in effect, been-nice-knowin'-ya? It was what *Sports Illustrated* would report:

> It wasn't until the moments immediately following the Blue Devils' 81–78 win over the Hoosiers, in the aftermath of Knight's well-publicized postgame brushoff of Krzyzewski, that Coach K finally read the letter. Its contents so undid him that he was unable to join his players at the press conference until he had a chance to compose himself.

The *Washington Post*'s Feinstein observed that Krzyzewski had been hurt by Knight's behavior but out of respect for the coach refused to criticize him. Feinstein then quoted an ex-Indiana player who said, in effect, Knight was tougher on his friends than his enemies.

Wrote Feinstein:

Friends must always toe the line; prove their loyalty over and over; deal with Knight's weird sense of humor and never, ever question anything he does. Knight is always testing everyone in his life— players, coaches, media members, friends, even family—and sometimes he goes too far.

A similar chill would develop years later when Steve Alford became a Big Ten coaching rival at Iowa. With Knight, it was his way or out-of-the-way. His autocratic nature had little flexibility. As his rigidity breached friendships, so did it box him into the combustible situation he would find himself in when the world saw that grainy tape of him choking Neil Reed.

It wasn't as if that moment with young Reed was Shock Theater. Knight had prepared his audience too well.

His son Patrick was a grade-schooler when dad had yanked Jim Wisman by the jersey, into a chair, to harangue him about bad passes.

Well, déjà vu to you, son. It was December 7, 1993, and Coach's kid, six-foot-six Patrick, a reserve on the Hoosier squad, had thrown a bone-headed pass in a game against Notre Dame. Never mind that Indiana led by 28 points at the time. The elder Knight was livid. He grabbed his son, pushed him into a chair and, before rebuking him, either kicked the chair Patrick was sitting on *or* kicked the boy himself.

To the Assembly Hall crowd occupying the seats behind the Indiana bench, it sure looked as if the the coach had lost his cool and kicked the boy. These courtside fans—all Hoosier supporters—booed and shouted at the coach. Knight shouted back at them in his usual profane language and for that—not the kick—was suspended for one game by I-U athletic director Clarence Doninger.

Afterward, Knight would say of Patrick, "I threw him into a seat. I've done this with other players. Then, like I often do, I kicked the side of the chair to get his attention. But to kick my son, no, I did not kick my son."

But at the game, his ex-wife Nancy was seen crying on the shoulder of Notre Dame Coach John MacLeod.

Patrick Knight? "I know he was going for the chair," he said. "My leg just happened to be where the chair was."

Later that season, on March 9, 1994, against Michigan State, Coach lost it again. This time the player incurring his wrath was no blood kin. A six-foot-four freshman, Sherron Wilkerson, committed three mistakes in a row and was relegated to the bench. As Knight, standing over him, began his tirade, he leaned toward the player and head-butted him—creating another golden moment for ESPN SportsCenter replay.

As ever, Knight had his version. He said it was an accident that their heads had clashed—he had only meant to lecture the player.

Wilkerson, sounding as if he was suffering from Stockholm Syndrome, said: "When it [the head butt] first happened I was kind of mad because I didn't know what it was for. When I found out what it was for, after I had time to gather myself and think about it, I'm kind of glad he did it, whether it was on purpose or an accident. Myself? I think it was an accident." (Wilkerson would transfer to Rio Grande College in 1994.)

Wilkerson's teammate and the Hoosiers' leading scorer, Damon Bailey, said, "I don't see what the problem is. We're the ones. Sherron's the one that's getting head-butted, or Pat's the one that happens to be kicked, or this guy's the one that gets pushed or whatever happens. If we understand what he's doing, if we understand that he's just trying to make us a better player, that's just coach's way of doing things. Different coaches have different styles. What we can't figure out is why everybody worries about it when it's us he's dealing with and not everybody else."

That did not suffice as reason to leave Knight alone. For his critics, wrong was wrong, whether the victim went along with it or not. In *USA Today*, columnist Bryan Burwell uttered what had by now become a refrain: it was time to fire Knight.

> Knight, increasingly incapable of staying on the right side of that fine line between authority and abuse, has become the Woody Hayes of college hoops. He is a liability. An embarrassment to the sport and the university. All the trophies, all the victories no longer offset the stupidity. Fire him.

More and more these days Knight was compared with Hayes, that symbol of temper gone amock. The ticking time bomb detonated. And yet, even as he "acted out," even as he clearly could not control himself, Knight carried on with hardly a peep from on high. Ehrlich had been chastened. He'd quickly found out about priorities at I-U, Knight putting him in his place with his New Mexico flirtation . The emperor of hoops reigned.

The only resistance—the only sign that enough was enough—would come from his team. See, in the past, Knight had had players defect from his program. But by 1997 as the team had begun to malfunction in NCAA postseason play, the athletes who left —Neil Reed, Jason Collier—were serious players. And when they left, both let it be known that they'd had a bellyfull of Bobby Knight. They'd gone elsewhere to find a game that came with the occasional smile.

"I've been kicking myself for not coming [to Georgia Tech] in the first place," Collier said. "I appreciate this more because of what I've been through. I'm having fun, and I love it here. I told the guys, 'You don't know how good you have it. I know guys who would kill to be here.'

"I was never encouraged to be better at Indiana. It was the constant yelling and screaming that got to me. It was like your old grandmother nagging at you."

Reed experienced the same let-down: "As a kid, you look at Indiana and say, Wow, I want to play there. But then you get here and find out what it's really like. It wears you down and eats you up. I don't care what anyone says: There isn't anyone on that team who doesn't dread going to the gym to face him every day. . . . When you play for Coach Knight, you're not concerned with getting better. You only worry about surviving."

Both Collier and Reed would be rebutted, and disparaged, by Knight's lieges. But the defection of Luke Recker, well—that would be harder to explain away for even the most die-hard Knight supporter.

Recker was six-foot-six, a reknowned Indiana high school star with a Chip Hilton image—a nice white kid who had game. He was a fundamentally sound player from DeKalb High who figured to fit nicely in the team-oriented game Knight preached. But at the end of his freshman year, Recker approached Knight and told him he wanted to transfer.

According to the televised CNN/SI report that in time would beget Myles Brand's zero-tolerance declaration, "Knight blew up, threatened to resign, told his coaching staff to find new jobs and told Recker it was all his fault."

"After he talked to coach Knight," teammate Richard Mandeville said, "he came to my house and was just a mess. Luke was a mess. Oh, my god, he felt like he was going to ruin all the assistant coaches' lives, the program, the state of Indiana. He thought if he left, he would probably never be welcomed back to Indiana."

Knight recognized the public-relations hit he would take for losing Recker and, the CNN/SI report said, told the player he would lighten up—give his guys more breathing room. Recker stayed his sophomore year, averaged 16.2 ppg, but apparently felt dissatisfied still with the I-U program. This time he waited until Knight was away at a coaching clinic in Cuba to announce, through a late-night fax, that he was leaving I-U.

Unlike Reid and Collier, he did not express negative emotions about Knight. In a press release sent through DeKalb High School, Recker said:

It is with sincere regret that I am announcing today my decision to transfer from Indiana University. This is the toughest decision I have ever made. I love the state of Indiana, and playing for I-U was always my lifelong dream. It is not easy to leave my friends, my family, and my home state. I love to play basketball, and the thought of sitting out a year kills me. I appreciate the opportunity given to me by Coach Knight. However, I have not been satisfied with my development as a player. I blame no one but myself for this, and believe my development will best be

served in another program. I will be
weighing my options over the next few
weeks, and have made no decision as to
my next school. I would like to thank the
great fans of Indiana University basketball, and the entire community of students,
faculty and administrators for their support and friendship. I would also like to
thank the media for their generosity to me
over the years. Finally, I especially want
to thank my teammates. I love them all,
and will miss them greatly. Thank you.

While Recker's statement absolved Knight,
those who covered the college game were not
fooled. As Mike Decouroy of the *Sporting News*
would note:

Recker blamed his troubles at Indiana
on himself. But there is no question why
few elite players consider joining the Hoosiers, and why so many who do leave
ahead of schedule. The issue is not
whether Knight yells, swears or gesticu-
lates too much along the bench. Other
coaches yell. The difference is in how
players are made to feel about themselves
and their place in the program. Those who

have escaped Indiana say the pressure engendered by Knight was relentless and oppressive.

Recker transferred to Arizona, but soon after was in a car crash that left his girlfriend, Kelly Craig, paralyzed, her brother Jason in a coma and Recker himself with a broken hand. To be closer to his girlfriend's home, he then transferred to Iowa, where Steve Alford was coaching.

Meanwhile, events were conspiring to bring Coach to that fateful walk to Myles Brand's campus residence, with his future as Hoosier coach hanging in the balance.

Bobby Knight pleading his case. After nearly three decades as the emperor of Bloomington, who would have thought it would come to that?

16

Endgame

On May 15, 2000, Myles Brand, a gray-haired teacher of philosophy for 28 years, stood before a room crowded with media that were curious to learn the fate of the bad-boy coach. Knight did not appear at the session. While his fate would be revealed, he sat in his second-floor Assembly Hall office, answering mail.

Brand, who earned $272,0000 a year as Indiana's president, began his statement:

"In early March, I asked trustees John Walda and Fred Eichhorn to come to take a very difficult and important task for the university. They agreed to investigate the allegations of a former player, Neil Reed, which were made in a television report. I chose these two men because of their impeccable integrity, their strong devotion and knowledge to Indiana University, and because of their professional backgrounds as successful trial attorneys.

"As you know, Mr. Reed alleges that he was choked by coach Knight. This is a serious allegation. Trustees Walda and Eichhorn have conducted a seven-week, exhaustive investigation. This was done in the glare of public media attention, and it came to an end yesterday.

"The trustees have gathered ample information to make a thorough assessment of these issues. Indiana University, its family, its friends, its community, owe Mr. Walda and Mr. Eichhorn a great debt of gratitude. I'd like to now ask Mr. Walda to describe the investigation and the conclusions."

Walda, who was from Fort Wayne, stepped forward and told the gathered listeners: "On March 23 of this year, trustee Fred Eichhorn and myself were asked to conduct an investigation of certain allegations that had been made by former Indiana basketball player Neil Reed regarding his experience at Indiana University. Those allegations included one that he was choked by coach Bob Knight, that President Myles Brand was verbally abused and ejected from a practice, and that coach Knight had displayed soiled toilet paper in a heated discussion with players in the locker room.

"We began the investigation shortly after we were asked. Our investigation was conducted with the assistance of an experienced, licensed private investigator who assisted Mr. Eichhorn and myself in conducting the interviews.

"An attempt was made to contact all of the witnesses to the events that were described and which I have enumerated. In a few instances, individuals were gone; we couldn't contact them. There were a few individuals who would not cooperate with the investigation. In the end, however, I believe that each of the investigations with regard to these incidents has been conducted thoroughly, and I believe that there are no important pieces of evidence that have not been reviewed and considered for a final report.

"At this time, 29 individuals have been interviewed regarding the allegations. Twelve of them were employees of the Indiana University athletic department, or part of the Indiana University basketball staff. Nine other individuals were student-managers or trainers, and seven of those interviewed were former Indiana basketball players. In addition to the interviews, we analyzed a videotape of a basketball practice that apparently occurred in early 1997. The process by which that videotape became available is now well known. In addition, a forensic video expert has analyzed that videotape. This expert has more than 28 years of high-level experiences in reviewing and analyzing video content. After examining the video in question, he concluded that it was authentic, that a frame-by-frame review shows no evidence of any relevant action being removed or inserted.

"It indicates there is contact to the neck of the individual, Neil Reed, being confronted by coach Knight. It appears that there is a grab. It is clear, the expert has explained to us, that the action was a grabbing of the neck, not just as grabbing of Mr. Reed's shoulder or jersey. The elapsed time for the contact is 2.3 seconds.

"As a result of these interviews and of the investigation, including the videotape, we have reached certain conclusions with regard to the incidents described.

"First, we could not accurately determine if a locker room incident concerning soiled toilet paper actually occurred. Each witness was asked about that particular incident. Many claimed that this incident wasn't real, that it was a legend.

"Our investigation also found that President Brand was not dismissed from practice, as has been alleged. Nearly all witnesses, with the exception of two or three, claimed that they had never seen such an incident, but they'd only heard about it in the rumor mill.

"And the final incident, which is the most serious: Our videotape analysis, we conclude, has confirmed that Neil Reed was grabbed at the neck. He was not injured, but this action by coach Knight was clearly inappropriate and one which cannot be tolerated. This review is the first of its kind during coach Knight's 29-year tenure. It also uncovered new information that illustrated a protracted and often troubling pattern in which coach Knight has a problem of controlling his anger and confronting individuals. In order to ensure the integrity of the review, we promised at the beginning that all of those who were interviewed would be interviewed with confidentiality, and we intend to stick with that and therefore can't get into all details on the incidents that I'm referring to.

"Unfortunately, or fortunately, many of the details of these incidents have been widespread and have gotten much attention, so you know what most of them are. What we found was a lengthy pattern of troubling behavior by coach Knight.

"The trustees of Indiana University are primarily concerned with the fortunes and reputation of this university that we love so much. Our goal is to protect and enhance the image of Indiana University. And because that is our goal, we will not tolerate conduct from any persons who work for us that we consider to be embarrassing or that does not live up to the high standards that we expect of all who represent our university.

"Therefore, we are resolved that if coach Knight persists in the kind of conduct which we've discovered, it will not be tolerated. And as I said earlier and I reiterate now, there are no sacred cows in Indiana University, and this certainly includes the basketball program."

At this point, Brand stepped forward to say: "During my tenure at Indiana University since 1994, the issue of allegations that became known have been dealt with appropriately and investigated. But viewed by themselves, each allegation does not individually rise to the level of dismissal. But the review of the Neil Reed incident caused us to look at the sum total, the pattern of behavior, and from that perspective, it is troubling. This behavior cannot and will not continue or be tolerated at Indiana University. I believe coach Knight to be a man of integrity. We also have to remember that he has an illustrious career at Indiana University. His players have extraordinarily high graduation rates, and many of those young men have gone on to be excellent and productive citizens.

"On Saturday night, I spent a number of hours

with the coach, and he and I have had some discussions since then. In these discussions, he has given me his word that he will take extraordinary steps to change his behavior and represent Indiana University with honor and dignity. He has formally apologized and will do so to Jeanette Hartgraves, the administrative assistant to the athletic director, for a 1998 incident in which coach Knight verbally abused her.

"I've conferred at length with the I-U trustees, and they have delegated to me the responsibility of personnel decisions. Trustee Steven Ferguson recused himself from the beginning of these deliberations. And in the final deliberations, trustee Peter Obremsky also recused himself. Both because they have had legal dealings with the coach. I am acting then with the full concurrence of the remaining seven trustees. And after lengthy, very difficult deliberations, I recommended to the trustees that Bob Knight continue his duties as basketball coach, but I also recommended that he do so under very specific, very firm guidelines. And these guidelines and sanctions will send a clear message that abusive, uncivil, embarrassing behavior will not be tolerated.

"Let me read to you the directives and the sanctions: 'As a result of the review, which found a pattern of inappropriate behavior, the sanctions for coach Knight are a three-game suspension during the 2000–2001 regular season and a $30,000 fine. The fine will be withheld from his salary.

[Knight's I-U salary of $163,118 comprised a fraction of his annual earnings, which were supplemented handsomely by shoe and apparel endorsements and other auxiliary income sources.]

"'Two: Any verified, inappropriate physical contact with players, members of the university community or others in connection with the coach's employment at I-U, will be cause for immediate termination.

"'Three: Public presentations and other occasions during which coach Knight is a representative of Indiana University will be conducted with appropriate decorum and civility. Included among these are interactions with the news media. Any failure on coach Knight's part to meet these standards will be cause for further sanction, up to and including termination of his position as head coach of Indiana University's basketball team.

"'Four: A commission will be established to develop policies for appropriate behavior for all coaches, student athletes and the I-U athletic department employees. The code of conduct will outline sanctions for inappropriate behavior. The commission will be chaired by athletic director Clarence Doninger, and it will contain, among others, faculty members from the I-U Athletic Committee. The commission will make these recommendations to the Athletics Committee [and] to the president, for approval by the trustees.

"These sanctions and directives are effective immediately. The trustees and I are in absolute agreement: Should Bob Knight violate any of these requirements, he will be terminated. This is a zero-tolerance policy. If coach Knight had not agreed to all these steps, I would have recommended to the trustees that he be terminated now, and I believe the trustees would have concurred with that recommendation.

"Now this process has forced us to question how well Indiana University has handled the individual controversies and incidents in the past. Could these problems have been dealt with earlier and in a better way? The answer to the question is yes. I believe we could have dealt with them more effectively in the past.

"We have a systemic problem that allowed this persistent problem of unacceptable behavior to exist. In developing a strict code of conduct for all coaches, student-athletes and the athletic-department employees, we are taking our steps to rectify these systemic problems. We cannot change the past, but we can shape the future. Any coach or student-athlete who violates the code, including coach Knight, will face sanctions up to and including immediate termination.

"Now let me close my comments on a personal note. This has been an extraordinarily difficult and troubling process. On the one hand we are dealing with sensitive and very personal issues. Even more so, the trustees and I have had to deal with these issues in the spotlight of national attention. It has created an avalanche of responses from alumni, friends and some who don't know us at all.

"The media attention has focused on the negative aspects of Bob Knight's public career and his personality. There is a profound good side to him as well. Not only do his student-athletes graduate and they become good citizens, but that good side has been flawed by his temper. I have struggled, as have the trustees, to offer a balanced, tough, fair ethical solution in the light of what Bob Knight has been told in the past, and the directives he has had in the past, as well as the current situation. And I believe we have reached that conclusion. I'll turn it back to John [Walda] to read a statement now from the coach."

Walda told his audience: "Coach Knight has asked that the following message be conveyed on his behalf. It is dated today."

Knight's statement read as follows: "President Myles Brand, in a meeting with me, gave me a set of guidelines he expects me to follow if I want to continue as Indiana University's basketball coach.

"I have absolutely no problem with the guidelines. The establishment of effective and proper guidelines can, in the long run, help me become a better coach.

"As I have said before, I recognize that I have a problem with my temper. For those times it has ever caused me to do anything that gave anyone understandable and justifiable reason to be upset, I am sincerely sorry."

[Signed Bob Knight.]

So there it was: zero tolerance.

Bobby Knight was one false step from Woody Hayes-like infamy.

Knight's act of contrition—his appeal to Myles Brand on May 13—had saved his job.

Brand told newsmen that that night he had advised his controversial coach that he had the backing of the trustees to fire him if he chose to.

"And I think that was a shock to him," said Brand. "I don't think he had ever heard anything like that before."

But in their two-hour, late-night meeting, Knight had told him: "I want to coach at Indiana University. I'll do whatever it takes."

Brand—and the trustees—had bought Knight's promise.

"Before the meeting I didn't believe he could change his behavior," Brand said. "I'd never seen him before contrite and apologetic . . . sincere. He made a personal pledge to me to change his behavior. He gave me his personal word. And I believe him."

So Knight had survived—barely. Trustee Ray Richard would tell CNN/SI: "When I went into the final meeting at which we were going to make a decision, I was going to vote to fire him, and I think the majority of the trustees agreed with me."

Brand, the I-U philosopher-president, said, "Aristotle said you become virtuous by doing virtuous acts. What that means is virtue is not innate, but it is learned. And it is learned by creating habits, by doing the right things.

"And over time, as Coach's behavior becomes a habit of being civil, it will take much less effort for him. He'll learn. It's true of all people."

That roseate view of Knight—not to mention I-U's resolution of its seven-week investigation—

drew fire from near and far. As Knight was leaving for a two-week golfing vacation in Scotland, his detractors were raising holy hell that I-U had not fired him.

"WHITEWASH INDIANA CAVES, BOB KNIGHT STAYS" was the headline on the cover of *Sports Illustrated*, over a photo of angry Knight.

In a column formatted as a letter to Brand, a former Indiana alumnus, Steve Jacobson, wrote in Long Island-based *Newsday,* that he was planning on attending the 45th reunion of his graduating class and looked forward to showing his wife Bloomington landmarks like the tavern where Hoagy Carmichael wrote "Stardust" and I-U's Ernie Pyle Hall, where Jacobson had been sports editor of the *Daily Student.* He said he wished he could have congratulated Brand at that time for doing right by the school and firing Knight.

Perhaps I was asking too much when Coach Knight had been the department wagging the school so long. . . .

You said, "He has given me his word that he will take extraordinary steps to change his behavior." . . . Was I reading too much into his apology when he said, "I have always been too confrontational, especially when I know I'm right."

Jon Wertheim, who had grown up in Bloomington and been a rabid fan of Knight's Hoosier teams, would write on CNN/SI.com that I-U had blown it.

"I was ashamed for pusillanimous administrators afraid to stand up to "Il Duce," resigned to employ tortured Jesuitical reasoning to justify his continued employment. . . . My deepest chagrin and sympathy, though, were reserved for the coach himself. Like the great tragic heroes of literature, Knight has been beset by classic Aristotelian "fatal flaw," in this case a powerful speedball of rage, ambition and intransigence. As in literature, by allowing this flaw to grow unchecked, Knight has brought about his own downfall.

Bill Plaschke in the *Los Angeles Times* had this to say:

Presented with a nicely garnished chance to fire a coach who has outlived his methods and overplayed his madness, Indiana officials did what they always do in these situations. They listened to the coach. They kissed his red sweater. They ran his strange plays. In doing so, they behaved far worse than Knight has ever dreamed of behaving. They head-butted morality. They punched ethics. They choked dignity.

In the past, Knight had questioned the validity of sportswriters' analyses of him, insisting that without their having played basketball they hadn't the background, the authority to write about it. But that didn't apply to Bill Walton, who had played for John Wooden's UCLA teams and with the NBA Portland Trailblazers and Boston Celtics. Walton blistered Knight in an essay in *Time Magazine*, calling Knight "a dinosaur" and then conveying what Knight was like from a player's viewpoint:

> One thing that really stands out about Knight is that it's always about him. He's a lot like Dennis Rodman, with his calculated self-promotion. John Wooden was the antithesis of the anger, the scowl, the selfishness. With Coach Wooden, an Indiana native, life was always fun, always upbeat, always positive, always about the team, always about the greatness of the game.

> Knight represents the death of hope,
> the stifling control freak.

From the moment that Brand announced his zero-tolerance decision, the Knight story had been big news. For the *Indianapolis Star* it had merited front-page coverage—and seven full pages inside, 21 stories and columns in all.

And of course, it had incited sportswriters across the country to offer their perspectives on Knight's past and future.

From web sites like members.aol.com/rmk general, which billed itself as "The Dark Side of Bobby Knight", to late-night television, Knight was a hot topic. The day after Brand's announcement, David Letterman's Top Ten list was comprised of "Coach Bob Knight Tips for Controlling Your Anger." Among those helpful hints:

—"Don't choke anyone. If you must, make sure they deserve it."

—"Avoid situations that trigger outbursts—like being around people."

—"When your face turns the color of your sweater, take a time out."

On NBC, Jay Leno took his shot at Knight, too. In his monologue, Leno said, "It seems the

University of Indiana officials met yesterday and decided not to fire Bobby Knight. He didn't get canned. They say one reason Bobby Knight was not fired was so he could beat two all-time records. Dean Smith's record for all-time coaching wins and Albert DeSalvo's Boston Strangler record."

So it went. It was open season on Robert Montgomery Knight. Not that he hadn't his defenders. In Indiana, he was still a man of influence, still commanded the support of those rabid Hoosier fans. In fact, when his long-time university critic, Murray Sperber, continued to snipe at him after Brand's announcement, the Knight diehards snapped to. Sperber was forced to take a leave of absence from I-U after receiving death threats because of his negative comments.

In the national media, conservative types like Rush Limbaugh and Oliver North were quick to back the coach. And Bernie Miklasz in the *St. Louis Post-Dispatch* wrote:

> It shouldn't surprise me that so many sportswriters want to banish Knight now, banish him forever, without granting a last-chance shot. But it does, only if you compare the journalistic hostility to the sympathetic columns you see written in

New York over baseball players who are repeat drug offenders.

The trouble was that just when Bobby Knight thought it was safe to resurface, his past flamed up again. In the May 22nd edition of the *Tennessean,* a Nashville-based newspaper, Chris Lawson, who had played for Knight from 1989–91 before transferring to Vanderbilt, accused the coach of more past acts of abusive behavior toward his players.

Lawson, 29, a pharmaceutical salesman in Salina, Kansas, said that not only had Knight pelted him with basketballs at close range during a practice but that he had punched a player in the head at halftime of a 1990 game against Iowa State.

As *Tennesseean* reporter Jim Wyatt wrote:

Lawson refused to name the player specifically, saying only "he was another big guy" on the team. Lawson said the player hasn't come forward himself because of fear he'd be vilified. The player, with whom Lawson remains in contact, finished his career at Indiana.

He screwed up in the game, and at halftime Coach actually punched him in the head. It was a punch on the side of his head," Lawson said. "The same guy, in practice when he would make a mistake, Coach Knight would grab his shorts and kick him as hard as he could in the butt, and after practice there would be bruises and stuff.

When reporter Wyatt followed up by contacting six-foot-nine Matt Nover and asking whether he had been the object of Knight's displeasure at Iowa State, Nover said, "Whatever happened in that locker room was between all of us players and coaches. He [Knight] was upset with me like he has been with players in 1,000 games before, and like any other coach would be with any other player who was playing bad and not doing what he was supposed to do. We came off, and whatever happened in that game that he was angry with me for, he let me know it. In no way was I abused or hurt. He let me know that I was making mistakes, and we went back on the floor and continued to play the game."

Lawson said that when he had transferred to Vanderbilt, he had not spoken negatively about Knight for fear of being maligned as Neil Reed later was. But after seeing Knight get off with what Lawson felt was mild punishment, he decided to go public with his accusations.

"All that other stuff that's out there, that's just the tip of the iceberg," Lawson said. "There are a lot of people that could come forward with a lot of bad stuff, but they're afraid to say anything."

Of the time Knight lost his temper with him, Lawson recalled: "We were practicing, and I didn't get a rebound he thought I should have got, and he stopped practice. I stood at the free-throw line and he had a rack of balls that had maybe ten to fifteen basketballs on there, and he just took them and threw them at me as hard as he could from about 5 to 6 feet away. I'm sitting there thinking, 'I can't believe this is happening to me.' I started laughing and that made him even more upset. But how do you deal with that?

"There was just so much crazy stuff the whole time. I can't tell you how many doors were kicked in, coolers were smashed and VCRs broken, on top of everything else he did. . . . I hope more stuff comes out. He'll never get what he deserves."

The question now was whether this temperamental coach could operate under the constraints that I-U had set forth. It would not be easy. Given his past history, and new guidelines, he would be a target. It was not hard to imagine Knight being baited wherever he went—by newsmen whom he had disdained, by fans of rival teams, by civilians bent on provoking him if for no other reason than to be the one who could say he had pushed Bobby Knight over the edge. In an era of easy celebrity, that would be a negotiable accomplishment.

Then there were the potentially flammable situations involving basketball. Could Knight avoid the spontaneous combustion that had triggered the Neil Reed choking incident and other blow-ups with his players? And what about the questionable calls made by officials—could he control his reaction to them? Could he, in short, cease and desist as the ticking time bomb that friends and foes alike had watched with morbid fascination over the years?

When Knight returned from his vacation in Scotland, he agreed to be interviewed on ESPN by Roy Firestone and a longtime friend, Digger Phelps, who had coached at Notre Dame before becoming a TV commentator. The interrogation, it was assumed, would offer the public a chance to judge whether Knight was chastened at having been put on zero-tolerance notice by the university. Was his last-minute solicitation of President Brand—and the promises he had made to change his ways—for real? Or merely lip service, a ruse to keep his job?

And in this age of media spin, what ulterior motives could be glimpsed in having Knight appear on ESPN? John Feinstein facetiously called it "The Bob Knight Rehabilitation Tour"—a suggestion that Indiana University, and Knight, meant to show that Coach was a reconstituted soul, a man who would bear up under the glare of the perpetual spotlight. An image that might or might not reflect the reality of Bobby Knight.

The ESPN interview was scheduled for the evening of May 30, 2000. Earlier that day, Knight would sit with a group of seven favored reporters—Lynn Houser and Mike Leonard of the *Bloomington Herald-Times*, Dave Kindred of the *Sporting News,* William Gildea of the *Washington Post*, Ursula Reel of the *New York Post*, Billy Reed of the *Lexington* (Ky.) Herald-Leader and Hubert Mizell of the *St. Petersburg* (Fla.) *Times*—to discuss his situation, in what amounted to a dress rehearsal for the Firestone/Phelps interview.

If television viewers tuned in later expecting to see a contrite Knight, think again. Early on, the coach acknowledged his temper, saying: "I've understood for a long time, maybe way back when I was playing in high school, that temper is a problem for me."

Yet throughout the hour-long show, Knight would try to mitigate his history of misbehavior.

—"If you took the percentage of times that I have really gone overboard . . . that's a pretty small percentage of all the circumstances I've been in."

—"When I'm right about an issue, I don't handle it particularly well."

—"I think my own guidelines have been pretty good. When you consider the whole across-the-board contribution that I've made to basketball or the university, it's been pretty good."

Most startling was his reaction to the Neil Reed tape. Knight claimed not to have seen the tape in spite of its countless airings. When ESPN offered to show it, he declined, saying, "I don't need to. I looked at the tape probably twice after that practice was over."

Knight told Firestone he didn't have to review the tape because he knew he did not choke the player. "I've never choked anybody," said Knight. "If you take all of the allegations that were made prior to that tape being shown, and then you take exactly what took place on that tape and you compare the allegations, then you or anyone else can simply drawn their own conclusions."

Deny, deny, deny.

The conclusion that many observers drew was that Bobby Knight didn't really "get it."

Typical was the *Indianapolis Star* editorial that called him "the same ole, arrogant coach":

> Even when he acknowledged errors, there were excuses. "Am I any different than a lot of people?" he asked at the end of the session with Roy Firestone and Digger Phelps.
>
> "When I'm right about an issue, I don't handle it particularly well," he said, repeating an earlier claim that his emotional outbursts are somehow linked to being treated wrongly by refs or others.

New York Post columnist Phil Mushnick saw the same contrary coach, the *Star* did.

> Like a petulant child, Knight even suggested that the tape of him attacking Neil Reed's throat—the smoking gun—actually proved that he hadn't done what he'd been accused of doing, that he hadn't technically choked Reed.
>
> In the end, the new Bob Knight was the same old boorish Bob Knight. He insists on being treated with dignity while treating others with none.

What was left in the aftermath of Knight's verbal slip-and-slide, his kneejerk justifications was a coach confronting the beast within—doing it under changed conditions that required him now to tame that wild side or be fired. For nearly 30 years, Bobby Knight, a full professor in the department of health, physical education and recreation, had done as he pleased—he'd taught basketball with a perfectionist's standards and a short fuse. No more. Zero tolerance meant one misstep and he was gone. At least that's what Myles Brand had said. Could Knight handle that? Could the anger that had fueled his methods be contained? Could he survive in the white-hot spotlight, with folks everywhere watching him as if he were a circus sideshow?

On September 7, 2000, at about 2 P.M. came a preview of what awaited Coach-in-a-cage. On that day, Knight was walking into Assembly Hall with assistant coach Mike Davis when Kent Harvey, a 19-year-old I-U freshman who was on line to buy football tickets, hollered out, "Hey, what's up, Knight?"

What happened next was, as so often occurred in Knight's life, subject to conflicting versions.

Knight claimed he approached young Harvey and, putting his hand on the student's elbow, said the following to him: "Son, my name is not

Knight to you. It's Coach Knight or it's Mr. Knight. I don't call people by their last name, and neither should you."

Harvey's version, as first offered by his stepfather, Mark Shaw, was that Knight had grabbed the youth by the arm, whirled him around and began cursing him for being disrespectful.

Later, when interviewed by Indianapolis TV station WRTV, Kent Harvey would say: "I called him by his last name and he blew up. I froze. I didn't know what to say. I didn't know what to do."

Knight denied he'd been physical with Harvey or that he cursed him.

"I would have to be an absolute moron—an absolute moron—with the things that have been laid on me to grab a kid in public, or curse at a kid in public, as apparently it's been said I did," he said.

At a news conference Knight used a blackboard to show who did what and where.

"This was simply a matter of manners and civility," he told the media. "I don't think my voice ever rose above a conversational tone. This is what happened and that's entirely what happened and any deviation from that is absolutely inaccurate—completely inaccurate."

Davis backed Knight, saying the Shaw-Harvey version was "a flat-out lie."

"I told the police," said Davis, "that if they give everybody [Harvey's friends and brothers, who were with him at the time] a lie-detector test, I guarantee they'll fail.

"The grab was like shaking hands. It wasn't stern. I stopped and watched and then we all walked off. The kid was joking and laughing at it after. I was there."

But Shaw disputed the coach, insisting that Knight had left marks on his son's right arm from his insistent grip. It was Shaw who brought the incident to the university's attention by phoning Christopher Simpson, I-U's vice-president of public affairs.

In a news release, Simpson said the university was taking the allegations "extraordinarily seriously" but declined to comment further while the matter was being investigated by university police.

In pursuing his stepson's encounter with Knight, Shaw came under scrutiny. He was an attorney, an author and a former Bloomington-area radio talk-show host who had frequently criticized Knight. Was it sheer coincidence that his stepson had triggered an incident? Or was Mark Shaw a man in pursuit of a Larry King exposure?

Didn't matter. Over the 17 weeks since "zero tolerance" had been declared, Knight, it turned out, had been a contrary soul, acting as if he was still making the rules. The Harvey flare-up was just another proof that Knight didn't "get it." As the matter was being investigated, Brand asked Knight to postpone a Canadian fishing trip, but Knight, ever in character, refused. For Brand, that was it—it was time to cut the arrogant coach loose.

In this season of zero tolerance, just as sure as the leaves would turn colors soon and another basketball season would follow, so too would Robert Montgomery Knight find himself for the first time in decades on the outside looking in.

Tick, tick, tick, KA-BOOM!

Epilogue

Through all his controversies, Bobby Knight rarely admitted wrongdoing. There was always a story: He was misinterpreted, mistreated, misunderstood.

Two nights after he was fired as coach of Indiana, it was more of the same as Knight appeared for a 40-minute interview on ESPN with Jeremy Schaap.

Knight had explanations for the various incidents that Brand had said formed a pattern of unacceptable behavior over the previous 17 weeks. But the through-line of Knight's rebuttal was that he had been done in by an administration not in tune with Coach—and that zero tolerance was nothing but a ruse. His fate had been sealed back in May when Brand had fined him, suspended him for three games and said he had to change his ways.

"My mistake," he said "was overstaying the situation. The situation changed. The people changed. We have different philosophies. We even interpret words differently."

He claimed that attempts to have the particulars of "zero tolerance" explained to him by emissaries of Brand had failed to generate an answer. Point by point he gave his version of the various circumstances Brand had cited as behavioral lapses on his part since the school had put him on notice. Those allegations against him were a matter of "interpretation", or simply untrue, Knight said.

Who knows? Maybe the administration did have it in for Knight after all. Maybe zero tolerance was just another way to say no more. Didn't matter, really, who was telling the truth. Through those 40 minutes, the only certainty was that Knight meant to be Knight—ever in command, bulldogging his way through interviewer Schaap to give his side of things. And reacting in character when Schaap, the son of veteran TV sports host and journalist, Dick Schaap, sought to keep him from filibustering.

There came that moment in the interview when, as Jeremy Schaap tried to redirect Knight,

Coach became visibly peeved. He threw the young interviewer the *malocchio* and told him he had "a faculty for interrupting."

Then it got personal: "You've interrupted my answers with your questions. You've got a long way to go to be as good as your dad."

It was a bully's reflex, and it cried out, if only subliminally in the viewer's mind, that phrase that had recurred so often lately with the Coach: Anger management . . . anger management . . . Anger management—like the tilt sign on a pinball game. Whatever. Coach would be Coach again.

Somewhere, some time in the not too distant future, he would find another university in tune with his harmonies.

And the story would go on . . .

APPENDIX

Parting Shots:
Pro & Con

Gary Namie, a California psychologist and president of the Campaign Against Workplace Bullying: "Knight is the epitome of a bully, and a perfect example of the kind of behavior that needs to be reined in. Unfortunately, there's no law against being a bully." [2000]

Robert Byrnes, Indiana University history professor: "Bobby is the greatest teacher I have ever seen. If he were a history professor, he'd put us all to shame. The only hope I have is that somebody . . . can tell Bobby, 'You can be intense and demanding, and you can do it without the vile, unspeakable language and without the rude and barbarous behavior.' " [1979]

Tony LaRussa, baseball manager/friend of Knight: "No matter how times are different, some important principles never change. Coach Knight is right to insist on things like integrity when building a program. Ignore the cheap shots. Cut through the B.S. and remember what he stands for." [2000]

Jeff Turner, a member of Knight's 1984 Olympic squad: "The man is very demanding and a perfectionist. I don't think he will be happy until he coaches a team that wins, 100–0, the opposing team never gets off a shot and his team never commits a turnover. He was a lot different than C. M. Newton, my coach at Vanderbilt. . . . He was not a screamer like Bobby Knight. But that's Knight's style." [1984]

Michael Jordan, comparing Knight with his college coach, Dean Smith: "My coach, Dean Smith, and Coach Knight are about the same except for the language." [1984]

Damon Bailey, I-U player: "Coach Knight is not an easy person to play for, and some guys can't handle that. We get a lot of comments from people who were not successful when they were here and were not successful when they left." [2000]

Sam Smith, *Chicago Tribune:* "To me, he betrays his student-athletes. While he certainly encourages that they complete their degree requirements, he fails to realize college life is more than the paper it's printed on. It's been said that while education is a wonderful thing, nothing really worth knowing can be taught. It often has to be shown or seen. Knight fails here and he should be judged in that vein because he earns his money from a university." [1991]

Lou Henson, former University of Illinois coach, now coaching at New Mexico State: "He's a classic bully, I'll tell you. He intimidates the Big Ten office, he tries to intimidate everybody. His entire life is based on intimidation." [2000]

Delray Brooks, I-U player who transferred: "You're going to be pushed. You're going to be driven to the point where you don't think you can take it any more, but you can. He's going to play his way, and you're going to do exactly as he says or you're not going to play. There's not a lot of room for improvisation." [1999]

Edwin Williams, I-U administrator: "Bob always—always—has to have the last word. And more often than not, it's that last word that gets him in trouble." [1986]

Tom Barnidge, *The Sporting News*: "Bobby Knight is a guy who helps keep the earth spinning in place. He helps keep the forces in balance. His outrage balances nicely against the mature, decent souls on the planet." [1985]

John Feinstein, *Washington Post*: "This is a man who has won all the big coaching victories there are to win, not only on the court but off it. And yet, he still has to play mind games with people; still, for some reason, has to prove that he is in control every single day." [1993]

Pete Newell, coach: "He reminds me of the line from Bob Hope's song, 'Thanks for the Memories': 'You may have been a headache but you've never been a bore.' " [1985]

Patrick Knight, the coach's son: "We know coming in, when we sign a letter-of-intent, this is no circus. It's not going to be a carnival like a lot of other schools. We know what we're getting outselves into." [1994]

Landon Turner, I-U player: "There were times I was thinking of quitting Indiana University basketball and thank God I didn't. A lot of the problems I had with the coach was because of me. I was out chasing the young ladies and having a good time when you're supposed to be here to get a great education. If I was talking in church as a child, my father took care of me when we got home. And when I wasn't doing the right things here at I-U, my father at I-U put me in the doghouse." [2000]

Dave Anderson, *New York Times* columnist: "In his complex nature he is part Gen. George Patton, part Billy Martin, part Woody Hayes and part Dr. James Naismith, who invented the game that Bobby Knight teaches so well. If only Bobby Knight could teach himself to live with a controlled offense." [1981]

Frank Deford, writer: "As intelligent as Knight is about most things, as searching as his mind is, he's encumbered by a curious parochialism that too often brings him grief." [1985]

Jud Heathcoate, Michigan State coach: "Like the comment he made Saturday telling critics to kiss his behind. I could see it, I could even empathize. But why? Why? Why? It's not necessary, it's not easy to defend, and in all honesty, it's not called for. All of a sudden people who don't know the real Bobby Knight have ammunition." [1995]

Karen Knight, the coach's second wife: "I heard someone describe him one time as a man of substance in an age of style. I think that's true." [2000]

John Laskowski, I-U player: "The greatest thing about him is that he cares so much about his players. He cares about what we do when we graduated from school—if we are successful. Of course, he emphasizes basketball but he uses it to make us better people. But he doesn't care about anybody except the players—not the press, university or fans. He takes it upon himself to be the receiver of bad press and gives up his image to protect his players. We see him in a different way in our closed practices." [1976]

Richard Mandeville, I-U player: "The guys who leave that program make the best decisions ever. If I had to do it all over again, I would have left after my freshman year." [2000]

Gene Wojciechowski, the *Sporting News:* "His players might wear crewcuts, but this definitely isn't the 1950s." [1994]

James (Doc) Counsilman, I-U swimming coach—"He is the master coach—one of the finest minds to ever coach basketball. With the players he is a disciplinarian, but he also has a genuine interest in their welfare and a real affection for them. And, in return, he has their respect. He understands people and knows how to handle them—except for sportswriters and alums. He doesn't consider them as people." [1976]

Alan Henderson, I-U player: "He got on me sometimes like he got on everybody. But he knew I could take that and I never let it get me down and I just kept pushing through it. And now that I am done, we stay in touch. When I finished, he even wrote me a letter just letting me know how much he appreciated what I did for the program." [2000]

Mike Miday, I-U player who quit the team: "I really wanted to play for the guy, but just found out how he truly is. When you are recruited, you don't see him in a tense situation . . . he just goes bananas." [1976]

Harold Andreas, the high school coach who first hired Knight as an assistant: "He can be as charming as anybody in the world or he can be the biggest horse's ass in the world. But he makes

that decision, and he does it in a split second."
[1981]

Bill Walton, former college and pro player:
"Why is he so angry? It's a question that springs
to mind when I look at an image of Bobby Knight
in full fury. Apparently it's one that Indiana University's officials didn't bother to ask themselves
before they allowed this dinosaur to remain as the
school's basketball coach despite a well-documented history of abusing players, coaches, administrators and anyone else who just happened
to be there." [2000]

Myles Brand, from his 1984 book, *Intending
and Acting: Toward Naturalized Action Theory*:
"Sometimes actions are performed involuntarily,
which include those done from strong emotion or
instinct." [1984]

Steve Alford, I-U player: "I have a world of
respect for Coach Knight. He did a lot for me as
a player and a person. I owe him a great deal for
where I've been as a player and where I hope to
go as a coach. I wouldn't play for anyone else at
the college level. Coach Knight always was very
honest and very fair. To play at I-U , you've got
to be an individual who honestly wants to become

a better player and a better person. Everything
Coach Knight has done, he's been successful at,
and he's done it by the book. All of his players
graduate and a majority of them are very successful whether it's in the NBA or in private life."
[1999]

Larry Donald, *Basketball Times*: "Knight's
problem isn't so much his temper or how he handles things, but, instead, how he views life. To
understand his aloof, arrogant visage of the world
around him, you need do nothing more than look
at his appearance on game night. In a profession
where every major college coach is attired in a
suit or sport coat accompanied by shirt and tie,
Knight shows up looking like a guy who just got
off the late shift at a local factory and has come
over to coach a little CYO ball." [2000]

Rick Reilly, *Sports Illustrated*: "The worst
part is this: You'll let him get away with it, and
he'll win 117 more games and end up the winningest coach in college basketball history, which
would be akin to Jerry Springer's winning a Pulitzer. Knight ahead of Dean Smith? As a man,
Knight can't carry Smith's whistle. As it is,
Knight ahead of John Wooden stinks. Wooden
could think of something nice to say about Al Ca-

pone, but you bring up Knight's name and Wooden's mouth crinkles into a 'no comment.' " [2000]

Bill Benner, *Indianapolis Star*: "You wonder why it took a few seconds of grainy practice videotape to bring the I-U administration to this point. Did it take 29 years to notice that your basketball coach has been, on many occasions, not a very nice man?" [2000]

Indiana Governor Frank O'Bannon: "I think any time you have incidents where there's a lack of control of the temper, it gives coach Knight a black eye. What the leadership has done is say we must correct that and taken stern action to correct that." [2000]

Skip Bayless, *Chicago Tribune*: "Let the Barnum and Bobby Circus begin. The white haired bull in the red sweater will be prodded and poked like a caged animal. Bobby-baiting could be a fan.com contest, an Emmy category. Which sends Knight over the edge? Which reporter from which network can ask the question that finally pushes his eject button?" [2000]

Hubert Mizell, *St. Petersburg Times*: "Indiana University, with well-documented and deeply bruised reason, is demanding not only a new day but a new Knight. If the General can handle this, he should be coach of the year and front-runner for the Nobel Peace Prize." [2000]

Myles Brand on the day he fired Knight: "There have been many instances in the last 17 weeks in which Coach Knight has behaved and acted in a way that's both defiant and hostile. These actions illustrate a very troubling pattern of inappropriate behavior that makes it clear that Coach Knight has no desire, contrary to what he personally promised me, to live within the zero-tolerance guidelines we set out on May 15." [2000]

Ray Richardson, Indiana trustee: "In the end, Bob Knight's attitude was just no longer tolerable." [2000]

Mike Krzyzewski, former Knight player and presently Duke coach: "It's tragic." [2000]

Dick Vitale, ESPN analyst: "I only wish and hope and pray he would look in the mirror and simply say, 'Everyone can't be wrong. Maybe I should go for a little counseling and anger control. And really try to put this thing aside and beat it like so many work so hard to beat any problem," [2000]

Tony Kornheiser, *Washington Post*: "It is a cheap, crummy way for Knight to go out, ripe with the smell of agent provocateur, considering the identities of the people involved. Undoubtedly, that's why the sanctimonious Brand ticked off a list of toothless 'incidents' he said illustrated Knight's alleged refusal to adhere to Indiana's new rules: to build a fuller case against Knight than just this one dubious incident. But adults can't grab kids and get in their faces. Not your kid. Not my kid. Not some talk-show host's kid. Bob Knight had to know he couldn't put his hand on a kid—especially since it was putting his hand on Neil Reed that led to the outcry to begin with." [2000]

Steve Alford: "I have always seen Indiana University and coach Knight as one and the same." [2000]

Scott May, I-U player: "This is shocking news. It's a sad day for the program." [2000]

Jerry Tarkanian, Fresno State coach: "From the outside it seemed like everyone was trying to agitate him and create a problem for him." [2000]

Bob Kravitz, *Indianapolis Star*: "Read my lips (and this goes double for the Knight zealots): He did it to himself. Just the way we all figured he would. Just the way all the fans and journalists who saw through the Great Lie knew he inevitably would. . . . Those who believed Knight would change also sustain a firm belief in the Tooth Fairy." [2000]

Jon Saraceno, *USA Today*: "That he is a serial grabber and an unrepentant bully are symptoms of something amiss in Knight's character. . . . Knight never grew up." [2000]

Knight's Players
After Indiana

[Reprinted with permission from the Indiana 1999–2000 Media Guide & Yearbook, which covers developments in players' lives up to 1999.]

CLASS OF 1972

RICK FORD

B.S. in Physical Education, Masters. Rick went into coaching and is a teacher at Cascade High School west of Indianapolis.

JOBY WRIGHT

B.S. in Physical Education, Masters. Joby played in the NBA for Seattle and San Diego and the ABA for Memphis and Virginia. He then played in Europe. He returned to I-U in 1978 and completed undergraduate requirements. He went on to complete a master's while serving as an assistant coach to Bob Knight for nine years. Joby spent four years as head coach at Wyoming after spending three years as the head coach at Miami (Ohio.)

CLASS OF 1973

STEVE DOWNING

B.S. in Physical Education, Master's. The Boston Celtics' No. 1 pick in 1973, Steve played for two years including the 1974 NBA championship season. He then returned to work at Indiana University-Purdue University at Indianapolis where he earned his master's in counseling. He joined IU's Department of Intercollegiate Athletics in 1979 and is now an associate athletic director.

JERRY MEMERING

B.S. in Business. Following graduation, he returned to his hometown of Vincennes, Indiana, to head up his business, Memering Construction Co.

JOHN RITTER

B.S. in Business. John worked several years at Eli Lilly before working as a TV commentator and as an assistant under Bob Weltlich at Ole Miss. He now lives near Indianapolis and sells insurance.

FRANK WILSON

B.A in Zoology, M.D. Dr. Frank Wilson, orthopedic surgeon, specializes in sports-related injuries from his northside Indianapolis practice.

CLASS OF 1975

DR. STEVE AHLFIELD

B.A. in Biological Sciences, M.D. An orthopedic surgeon, Steve owns Ahlfield Sports Medicine Orthopedic Center in Indianapolis. He was chief medical officer for basketball during the Tenth Pan American Games in Indianapolis in 1987.

DOUG ALLEN

B.S. in Business, Master's. Doug has been with Yellow Freight since graduation. He now serves as the company's vice-president.

STEVE GREEN

B.A. in Biological Sciences, D.D.S. Dr. Green is a dentist practicing in Indianapolis. He pinch hits for John Laskowski as basketball commentator on the I-U Television Network. Green played four seasons in the ABA and a year in Italy before going to dental school.

JOHN KAMSTRA

B.S. in Accounting, CPA. Kamstra works as an accountant with the Cook Group in Bloomington.

JOHN LASKOWSKI

B.S. in Business. Laz played two years with the Chicago Bulls. After spending many years in the business world, Laskowski now works for the I-U Alumni Association. He is in his 21st year on the I-U Television Network.

CLASS OF 1976

TOM ABERNETHY

B.S. in Business. Tom played with Los Angeles, Golden State and Indiana before playing in Italy. He owns his own company, the Abernethy Company, in Indianapolis, which deals in industrial real estate, development and property management. He also owns the Indianapolis Basketball Academy, a training facility for the sport.

QUINN BUCKNER

B.S. in Administration. The Milwaukee Bucks' No. 1 selection, Quinn played for 10 years in the NBA with Milwaukee, Boston and Indiana. He is now a network television analyst. He was inducted into the I-U Athletic Hall of Fame in 1986.

JIM CREWS

B.S. in Business. Jim served eight years as an assistant coach under IU coach Bob Knight. He is in his 15th year as the head coach at the University of Evansville.

SCOTT MAY

B.S. in Education. The Chicago Bulls' No. 1 draft pick, Scott played with Chicago, Milwaukee and Detroit before playing several years in Italy. He now lives in Bloomington, where he owns his own company, Scott May, Inc. Like teammate Quinn Buckner, he has been inducted into the I-U Athletic Hall of Fame.

DON NOORT

B.S. in Management. Don elected to concentrate on his degree his senior year and is now with a paper company in Lexington, Kentucky.

BOB WILKERSON

B.S. in Physical Education. He was drafted in the first round by Seattle and played with the Sonics, Denver, Chicago and Cleveland during his NBA career. He finished his degree in Indiana and at the University of Colorado. He now lives in Anderson, Indiana, and works with the Boys and Girls Clubs.

CLASS OF 1977

KENT BENSON

B.S. in Recreation. The Milwaukee Bucks took Kent as the No.1 pick in the 1977 draft. He played for them, Detroit, Utah and Cleveland before playing in Europe. A 1989 I-U Athletic Hall of Fame inductee, he now resides in Bloomington where he works with Diversified Benefit Services.

CLASS OF 1978

WAYNE RADFORD

B.S. in Business. Wayne played one year for the Indiana Pacers. He now works at the Cook Group in Bloomington.

JIM WISMAN

B.S. in Business. Jim spent four years with Cummins Engine Co., in Columbus, Indiana, and is now a vice president with Leo Burnett Advertising in Chicago.

CLASS OF 1979

SCOTT EELS

B.S. in Recreation. Scott is part of the Cook Group in Bloomington.

CLASS OF 1980

BUTCH CARTER

B.S. in Business. After serving as the interim head coach of the Toronto Raptors at the end of last season (1998–99), Butch was named the permanent head coach of the team. He played with Los Angeles, Indiana, New York and Philadelphia during his NBA career.

MIKE WOODSON

B.S. in Recreation. The New York Knicks' No. 1 pick, Woodson played for the Knicks, New Jersey, Sacramento, the Los Angeles Clippers and Houston during his 13-year career. He is now an assistant coach with the Milwaukee Bucks.

CLASS OF 1981

GLEN GRUNWALD

B.S. in Business, J.D. Glen completed his law degree at Northwestern and practiced law for several years with the firm of Winson & Strawn in Chicago. He is now general manager of the NBA's Toronto Raptors. He has also worked as a legal counsel for the Denver Nuggets.

PHIL ISENBARGER

B.S. in Business, J.D. Phil completed his law degree at the I-U School of Law in Indianapolis and is a partner in the Indianapolis firm of Bingham, Summers, Welsh and Spilman.

ERIC KIRCHNER

B.A. in Journalism. Eric is with Emery Worldwide where he serves as their Western Area Vice President. He works in Hayward, California.

STEVE RISLEY

B.S. in Business. Steve is completing his 10th year as a sales representative with Pfizer Pharmaceuticals after serving as a public affairs assistant for Dan Quayle, then a Republican junior senator from Indiana.

RAY TOLBERT

B.S. in Recreation. New Jersey's No. 1 draft pick, Ray played for the Nets, Seattle and Detroit during his NBA career before playing in Italy. He then played one year in the CBA before returning to the NBA with the Lakers and Atlanta. He is now a minister.

CLASS OF 1982

LANDON TURNER

B.S. in Physical Education. A tragic car accident ended Landon's playing career. He now lives in Indianapolis, where he is a motivational speaker. Turner received the 1989 Coors Light U.S. Basketball Writers Most Courageous award after returning to the court with a wheelchair basketball team.

CLASS OF 1983

STEVE BOUCHIE

B.S. in Education. Steve is part of his family's agricultural business in Washington, Indiana.

TONY BROWN

B.S. in Business. Tony lives in Chicago and is president of Fuci Metals, one of the largest metal companies in the world. He completed his degree work in 1985,

TED KITCHEL

B.S. in Management & Administration. After working in insurance in Kokomo and Indianapolis, Ted is now employed as a sales representative for Foot Joy in Cincinnati. He also handles the color commentary for Indiana basketball television broadcasts.

ISIAH THOMAS

B.A. in Criminal Justice. Isiah played 13 years for the Detroit Pistons and helped lead them to two World Championships. As his professional career permitted, Isiah completed classwork for his degree, which he officially finished in 1988. After serving as the Vice President for Basketball Operations and part owner of the NBA's Toronto Raptors, he now works for NBC on the network's NBA telecast. During the summer of 1999 he purchased the Continental Basketball Association.

JIM THOMAS

B.S. in Forensic Studies. Jim spent three years with the Indiana Pacers and then played in the CBA. He is now an assistant coach for the NBA's Toronto Raptors.

RANDY WITTMAN

B.S. in Management & Administration. Atlanta's No. 1 draft pick, Randy played with the Hawks for five years before finishing his NBA career with Sacramento and Indiana. He is in his first season as the head coach of the Cleveland Cavaliers after spending five years as an assistant coach with the Minnesota Timberwolves.

CLASS OF 1984

CAM CAMERON

B.S. in Management & Administration. Cam is in his third year as head coach of the Indiana Football program. Prior to returning to Bloomington, he was assistant football coach at Michigan and with the Washington Redskins. He has completed his master's in athletic administration.

CHUCK FRANZ

B.S. in Computer Science. Chuck is associated with the Cook Group in Bloomington.

CLASS OF 1985

UWE BLAB

B.A. in Computer Science and Mathematics. Uwe was drafted by the NBA's Dallas Mavericks and then played for Golden State. He was selected Phi Beta Kappa his senior year. He played for Germany in the 1992 Barcelona Olympics. He now lives in his native country.

DAN DAKICH

B.A. in Telecommunications. After his playing days, Dan spent 11 years as an assistant under Bob Knight. He is in his third year as head coach at Bowling Green.

CLASS OF 1986

WINSTON MORGAN

B.S. in Public Recreation. Winston worked for Yellow Freight in Indianapolis before playing with professional basketball teams in Argentina,

Sweden and Portugal. He is now a Production Account Executive at GES Exposition Service in Las Vegas, Nevada.

STEW ROBINSON

B.S. in General Studies. Stew lives in Bloomington, where he is currently employed by Cook Inc. He completed his degree requirements in December 1993.

COURTNEY WITTE

B.S. in Public Affairs. Courtney worked for 11 years with the Indiana Pacers as the team's Basketball Video Coordinator and as a regional scout. He is in his second year in the same capacity with the Philadelphia 76ers.

CLASS OF 1987

STEVE ALFORD

B.S. in Marketing. After being taken in the second round of the NBA draft, Steve spent two years with the Dallas Mavericks before playing for Golden State. He is now head coach at the University of Iowa.

TODD MEIER

B.S. in Marketing. Todd has returned to his home state of Wisconsin. He is in management with an outboard motor company in Oshkosh.

DARYL THOMAS

Daryl is playing professional basketball in England, where he's been chosen England's Player of the Year. He plans on playing in Europe this year.

CLASS OF 1988

STEVE EYL

B.A. in Marketing. After working for three years as a sales representative with Baxter International Pharmaceutical and Hospital Supplies, Steve moved to Australia, where he is currently working and playing basketball.

DEAN GARRETT

Completing degree requirements. He was drafted in the second round by Phoenix. Dean played in Europe for nine years before returning to the U.S. and playing with the Denver Nuggets. He is now with the Minnesota Timberwolves.

KEITH SMART

B.S. in General Studies. Keith was drafted by the Golden State Warriors in the second round of the NBA draft. He played professionally in the NBA, CBA and overseas. He is in his third season as the head coach of the Ft. Wayne Fury of the CBA.

CLASS OF 1989

MIKE D'ALOISIO

B.A. in Arts and Sciences. He now lives and plays in Italy.

JOE HILLMAN

B.S. in Business. Joe earned his degree in finance and real estate before playing basketball in Australia. He now lives and works in Indianapolis.

TODD JADLOW

B.S. in Public Affairs. After receiving his degree in management, Todd played in Europe. He now plays in Argentina.

MAGNUS PELKOWSKI

B.S. in Business, B.A. in Arts and Sciences. Magnus earned a business degree in finance and a liberal arts degree in German studies with a minor in studio art. He now lives in Germany.

BRIAN SLOAN

B.A. in Arts and Sciences. Brian completed medical school and is now a doctor and lives in Indianapolis.

KREIGH SMITH

Kreigh is living in San Francisco, where he is in business.

CLASS OF 1990

JEFF OLIPHANT

B.A. in Arts and Sciences, with a double major in telecommunications and psychology. Jeff completed law school and is working in Indianapolis.

MARK ROBINSON

B.G.S. in Continuing Studies. After completing his degree in general studies, Mark worked as a counselor in a Houston drug rehabilitation center and is now living and playing in Manchester, England.

CLASS OF 1991

LYNDON JONES

B.G.S. in General Studies. Lyndon is employed by Cook, Inc., in Detroit.

CLASS OF 1992

ERIC ANDERSON

B.S. in Sociology. Eric played for two seasons with the New York Knicks. He has also played in Europe. He now lives in Indianapolis where he is in the auto industry.

JAMAL MEEKS

B.S. in Criminal Justice. Jamal is an assistant basketball coach at Bowling Green.

CLASS OF 1993

CALBERT CHEANEY

B.A. in Arts and Sciences. After earning a degree in criminal justice, Calbert was selected with the sixth pick of the first round of the NBA Draft by the Washington Wizards. He is now in his first season with the Boston Celtics.

GREG GRAHAM

B.A. in Health, Physical Education and Recreation. He earned his degree in sports management. Greg was selected with the 17th pick of the first round by the Charlotte Hornets. His rights were then traded to the Philadelphia 76ers. He has also played with New Jersey and Seattle before finishing last season in the CBA.

MATT NOVER

B.A. in Business. After playing a major role in the movie "Blue Chips," Matt has played in Japan, Switzerland, Portugal and Australia. He plans on playing in Japan this year.

CHRIS REYNOLDS

B.A. in Arts and Sciences. After earning a degree in criminal justice and Afro-American studies, Chris earned a law degree from IU. He has worked in the compliance office of Michigan State and is now in the athletic academic office at Western Michigan.

CLASS OF 1994

DAMON BAILEY

B.A. in Education. Bailey was a second-round draft pick of the Indiana Pacers. He plays with Ft. Wayne in the CBA.

PAT GRAHAM

B.A. in Criminal Justice. Pat is Director of Marketing for Progressive Health Rehabilitation in Evansville, Indiana.

TODD LEARY

B.A. in Sports Management. After earning his degree in sports management, he played in Europe but now lives in Indianapolis, where he is in commercial real estate with Premier Properties.

CLASS OF 1995

ALAN HENDERSON

B.A. in Biology. Alan was picked in the first round by the Atlanta Hawks and is now in his fifth year with the team.

PAT KNIGHT

B.A. in Health, Physical Education and Recreation. Pat worked with the NBA's Phoenix Suns and was an assistant coach with the CBA's Connecticut Pride. Last year he was the head coach of the IBA's Wisconsin Blast. This is his second season as an assistant coach at I-U.

CLASS OF 1996

BRIAN EVANS

B.A. in Sports Management. Brian was the 27th selection in the NBA Draft by the Orlando

Magic. He played three years in the NBA and is playing this year in Italy.

KEVIN LEMME

B.S. in Education. After playing his senior year as a walk-on, Kevin is a high school teacher and coach.

TODD LINDEMAN

B.A. in Resource Mangement. Todd played in the CBA last season and plans on playing in that league or the NBA this year.

CLASS OF 1997

HARIS MUJEZINOVIC

B.A. in General Studies. Harris played for his native country in the European Championships during the summer of 1997 and played in Croatia last year. This season he is playing in Italy.

CLASS OF 1998

ROBBIE EGGERS

B.A. in Sports Management. Robbie plans on playing in Europe or with Athletes in Action this season.

RICHARD MANDEVILLE

B.A. in Sports Management. Richard plans on playing in Australia.

CHARLIE MILLER

B.A. in Criminal Justice. Charlie is now playing professionally in Switzerland.

ANDRAE PATTERSON

B.A. in Criminal Justice. The 46th pick in the NBA Draft by the Minnesota Timberwolves. Andrae is in his second year with the team.

CLASS OF 1999

WILLIAM GLADNESS

B.S. in General Studies. William is playing in Europe.

ROB TURNER

B.S. in General Studies. Rob is playing in Europe.

FOOTNOTE: Two conspicuous developments for Knight's boys in the year 2000: Isiah Thomas was named coach of the Indiana Pacers and Butch Carter was let go as coach of the Toronto Raptors.

The Knight Line:
Career Stats

BOBBY KNIGHT, OHIO STATE VARSITY STATS

Year	Games	FG	FGA	PCT	FT	FTA	PCT	REB	PTS	AVG
59–60	21	30	74	.405	17	27	.630	42	77	3.7
60–61	28	54	136	.397	15	26	.577	77	123	4.4
61–62	25	35	89	.393	9	11	.818	38	79	3.2
TOTALS	74	119	299	.398	41	64	.641	157	279	3.8

BOBBY KNIGHT'S COACHING RECORD

Year/team	Wins	Losses	Pct.
65–66 Army	18	8	.692
66–67 Army	13	8	.619
67–68 Army	20	5	.800
68–69 Army	18	10	.643
69–70 Army	22	6	.786

Year/team	Wins	Losses	Pct.
70–71 Army	11	13	.458
71–72 Indiana	17	8	.630
72–73 Indiana	22	6	.786
73–74 Indiana	23	5	.822
74–75 Indiana	31	1	.969
75–76 Indiana	32	0	1.000
76–77 Indiana	16	11	.593
77–78 Indiana	21	8	.724
78–79 Indiana	22	12	.647
79–80 Indiana	21	8	.724
80–81 Indiana	26	9	.743
81–82 Indiana	19	10	.655
82–83 Indiana	24	6	.800
83–84 Indiana	22	9	.710
84–85 Indiana	19	14	.576
85–86 Indiana	21	8	.724
86–87 Indiana	30	4	.882
87–88 Indiana	19	10	.655
88–89 Indiana	27	8	.771
89-90–Indiana	18	11	.621
90–91 Indiana	29	5	.853
91–92 Indiana	27	7	.794
92–93 Indiana	31	4	.886
93–94 Indiana	21	9	.700
94–95 Indiana	19	12	.613
95–96 Indiana	19	12	.613
96–97 Indiana	22	11	.667
97–98 Indiana	20	12	.625
98–99 Indiana	23	11	.676
99–00 Indiana	20	9	.689

THE SCORE TO NOW:

- Three NCAA championships: 1976, 1981, 1987
- 24 NCAA appearances
- 5 NCAA Final Four appearances
- 11 Big Ten championships
- Coached 13 All-Americans
- 14 of Knight's players have been first-round NBA Draft selections
- Coach of 1984 gold-medal U.S. basketball team
- Named Coach of the Year four times: 1975, 1976, 1987, 1989
- Voted into National Basketball Hall of Fame, 1991
- One of two coaches to win NCAA championships as a player and coach (Dean Smith is the other)

Knight's Hoosier Chronology

1971 Appointed coach at Indiana

1976 His undefeated team wins NCAA championship

1979 Convicted in absentia for hitting a policeman during Pan Am Games in Puerto Rico

1981 Wins NCAA championship again, but gets into scuffle with LSU fan before championship game

1984 Coaches U.S. Olympic basketball team to gold medal

1985 Throws chair after objecting to referee's call

1987 Wins his third NCAA title

1988 Pulls team off court with 15 minutes remaining during an exhibition game against a team from the Soviet Union. (Later in the year, tells Connie Chung of NBC-TV: "I think that if rape is inevitable, relax and enjoy it.")

1991 Voted into Basketball Hall of Fame

1992 Gives mock whipping to black player

1993 Booed by courtside fans for kicking his son, Patrick, while lecturing him during game

1994 Accused of head-butting a player while chewing him out during game

1995 Reprimanded and fined $30,000 by the NCAA for a profane outburst at a postgame news conference in the NCAA tournament

1997 Chokes Neil Reed for 2.3 seconds

1998 Fined $10,000 by the Big Ten for berating an official

2000 Investigated after Reed incident made public. That May 15, fined and suspended by university president, Myles Brand, who announces a "zero tolerance" policy for coach

On September 10, fired by Brand

About the Author

PHIL BERGER, award-winning journalist, author and screenwriter, has been covering sports and entertainment since the late sixties.

From 1969 to 1970, Berger traveled with the New York Knicks basketball team, and his warts-and-all account of the season, *Miracle on 33rd Street: The New York Knickerbockers Championship Season*, generated controversy. Although the Knicks barred him from the locker room for the next season, the book established his reputation as a sportswriter and secured him assignments from magazines like *Playboy*, *Penthouse*, *Esquire*, *Sport*, *Inside Sports*, the *Village Voice*, *Men's Journal*, *Look*, and the *New York Times Magazine*.

From 1985 to 1992, Berger was the *New York Times*'s boxing reporter, covering the sport's biggest names while authoring *Blood Season: Tyson and the World of Boxing* and a collection of his boxing profiles, *Punch Lines: Berger on Boxing*.

In 1990, *Big Time,* Berger's novel loosely based on the life of basketball rogue Jack Molinas, was published.

In 1993, Berger left the *Times* to write books and screenplays. He collaborated on the autobiographies of former heavyweight champions Smokin' Joe Frazier and Larry Holmes.

Among his other books are *Forever Showtime: The Checkered Life of Pistol Pete Maravich; Twisted Genius: Confessions of a $10 Million Scam Man* (with Craig Jacob) and *Deadly Kisses* (a novel).

Berger's movie script, *Price of Glory,* is the story of Arturo Ortega, a failed prizefighter who raises three sons to fulfill the dream of glory in the ring. Starring Jimmy Smits as Arturo, *Price of Glory* was released by New Line Cinema in March 2000.